UNSOLICITED ADVICE

from an

UNQUALIFIED SOURCE

Unsolicited Dating Advice from an Unqualified Source

Copyright ©2018 by Anthony Massey

ISBN 9781980612216

Published by The Mass Creative Group www.themasscreativegroup.com

Printed in the United States of America

UNSOLICITED ADVICE

from an

UNQUALIFIED SOURCE

TONY MASSEY

CONTENTS

ACKNOWLEDGEMENTS

To Mary, Tamela, and Mimi; thank you for soliciting my advice and making me feel qualified to give it.

To my son, Jordan and my mom; thank you for being the generational push to empower me to chase my dreams and live in God's purpose for my life.

To my incredible family; your love inspires me to be better.

INTRODUCTION

So you made the decision to start dating, or you've been dating and realized very quickly something you've always known: you suck at dating. Don't worry... you're not alone.

Cupid's arrow has hit every target around you and has, at the very least, wounded a few of your friends and family members. The little guy seems to avoid you like the plague and you're getting sick of it. So, you've sought assistance, advice, anecdotal wisdom, and you've even contemplated witchcraft to help you meet a nice, normal guy. You've almost bought into the lie that good guys don't exist or even worse that you will have to take whatever you can get. To quote the often misunderstood performer, Flavor

Flav: "don't believe the hype."

You've read books, listened to CD's, DVD's, MP3's and even watched a few VHS tapes from the early 90's in hopes of reliving those days when dating was just so much easier. You've followed the so called dating rules and you've even allowed yourself to be convinced that you should think a certain way and then act a totally different way. Despite all of the well intentions from friends and the slightly pervasive advice of family, you are still drowning in the dating pool!

In fact, the only thing you have gained thus far is a doctorate level education on sociopaths, liars, cheaters, and sex-obsessed mamma's boys who behave like children. So you ask yourself: "What's the problem?" The honest answer: "You...per se."

See, when it comes to dating, you like many women are just doing it wrong. There's absolutely nothing wrong with you but you are definitely going about this thing in all the wrong ways. Whether you believe that loves is a result of luck, fate, serendipity or divine intervention, there is one fundamental truth that must exist for you to find the love you seek. There's one secret that is actually well known and extremely popular, and it was probably the first and best piece of advice you received when you first voiced your desire for the cute boy at school to notice you. Somehow you forgot and I'm here to remind you!

Let me give you a little advice about advice: The worst advice is from anyone who suggests that a woman must change who she is for the purpose of meeting a man. Let me be clear, self-improvement is always a noble endeavor, as long as the motivation is pure. Changing a belief, thought process, or core value for the purpose of finding a man is not only reckless, it's a complete and total waste of time.

These pages are filled with my experiences, not my expertise. I am the product of a large matriarchal family, filled with women. These women and other female friends have shared their stories, anecdotes, and nightmares in the dating world with me over the years. Some have asked for my advice and my perspective as a man, and others have received both despite their objections.

My goal is to start a conversation, not to present myself as an authority figure. I believe that dating as an adult can be simplified if communication is improved. Men and women have different experiences, thought processes, and preferred methods of receiving and interpreting information. Often times, it is misunderstandings or lack of understanding that makes dating so difficult.

This book was written for women over thirty-five who are currently dating or considering dating. I believe that dating under thirty years old has a different set of rules and expectations, but a younger person who wants practical solutions for navigating the trepid waters of dating definitely can glean something from this book.

What This Book Isn't

This book is not a *how to guide* on getting a man or keeping a man. Quite honestly, in my opinion, any dating book written by an author that suggests he or she has this type of knowledge is a waste of paper. This book is also not an attempt at using reverse psychology to manipulate the female reader. You will not find any tricks or gimmicks on these pages. You will also not find any judgment. I made every attempt to write from the experience of a man who has dated and not an authority on dating. I hope this book is void of misogynistic and condescending advice that suggests a woman must change who she is in order to be with a man.

As a matter of fact, what you will find is my insistence that you are perfect the way you are. Any improvements, modifications, or changes that you decide to make should be motivated purely by your desire and no one's suggestion or pressure. Read every word of this book with an open mind and a measure of skepticism. Understand that you have choice and that choice should drive your decisions based on your personal beliefs, ethics, and standards.

At the end of each chapter you will find homework that will assist you in the process of self-examination and determining what you are looking for in a dating experience and your motivation for dating. As an instructional designer by trade, I feel it is important to receive information for the purpose of knowledge and practical application. Otherwise, it takes up precious space in your thoughts that could be better suited for something else. At the end of the book, you should have a very detailed description, written by you, of what you want, who you are, and how you should proceed in the wonderful world of courtship.

Finally, I acknowledge that advice is at its best fickle. Most advice books are written with broad, anecdotal dribble that does not dive deeper than the surface of any issue. Self- appointed gurus spout clever analogous quotes that barely hold truth to the most diverse audience. Most of the so-called advice is information that is well known, or at the very least common sense, packaged in fluff. The reality is that no solution has universal application and most advice books and tips are basically suggestions that women turn their backs on their true selves to compete for men. You won't find that here. I have no idea what it takes to get a good man. Hell, I can't with a hundred percent certainty say that I am a good man. However, I do know that women often make compromises and sacrifices for men who deserve neither. My desire is for the reader to make it to the end of this book with insight on dating and possibly achieve insight on who she is and how presenting her true self to a deserving man could result in a satisfying dating experience or possibly a long term, meaningful relationship. I have no secrets and I present no rules. Nothing contained in these pages is groundbreaking or life altering. These are the mistakes I made as a man and the lessons I learned from the women in my life. Enjoy.

INTRODUCTION

DATING: THE POINT OF IT ALL

No matter how love-sick a woman is, she shouldn't take the first pill that comes along – Joyce Brothers

Dating actually has a well-defined and specific purpose. Historically, the selection process of a potential suitor didn't really involve the woman or the man. Families selected suitable mates that provided financial and social benefits. Even in arranged marriages, there was still a season of courtship. Usually courting took place under the watchful eye of a parent or guardian and it consisted of talking and very little physical contact. In the mid-1800's courting couches, strategically crafted to create space between young lovers, were utilized to ensure a less salacious encounter. By the late 1800's and early 1900's a significant change occurred that now resembles the more current dating climate – women were given choice. A mate was no longer chosen and the subsequent courtship didn't always automatically end in marriage. A woman was now able to entertain a number of partners before making a final decision of who she would spend her time and life with. This, of course, created a competition for a woman's attention and ultimately her heart.

Smart men followed the unwritten rules of dating by presenting themselves in a polished and chivalrous manner. They vied for a woman and actively pursued her with the understanding that she could choose anyone she wanted. Still, women were subjected to a certain social order that was limiting and a bit stifling. This all changed in the wake of women's suffrage. Women demanded and ultimately received a persistent and piercing voice that would not be ignored for years to come. Women now had choice and power.

The rules of courtship have been slightly altered but unchanged. Women are now more capable than ever before and many have shown that given the chance, they can reach a level of excellence that exceeds any man. The change in the social order has made dating a bit more tedious, but not impossible.

Liberation can be quite daunting. Most of the women that I know are extremely successful and very independent. The women in my life are strong and very opinionated. In what seems like a dichotomy (but truly is not) all of them enjoy the traditional role of being a woman. They want to be pursued but not accosted. They want to be coveted and not controlled. They want to be comforted and not treated like a frail, infant. They want a man who can provide security and not psychotic rage. They want a man to know when it is important to open the door and when it is appropriate to allow them to enter into a space without any assistance. Basically, they want what they want exactly how they want it.

Unfortunately, they somehow believe it's a man's job to just figure all that out. Most of the men I know who are dating are just plain confused and none of them are mind readers.

There's an unfortunate phenomenon that takes place in our youth. We teach our daughters to be independent and our sons to be depended upon. We tell our daughters that they don't need a man and tell our sons to prepare themselves to be the head of a house. With these conflicting messages in tow, men and women enter the dating world with a complete misunderstanding of what to expect from each other.

Dating is an excellent opportunity to learn more about a person and see them in a variety of social settings. You need to see how he behaves in certain social situations to ensure you are getting an accurate view of who he truly is and not just the person he is trying to show you. We all send our best selves to the first date, at least we should.

My good friend Ebony was approached by a man in a shopping mall. The man presented himself well and Ebony was immediately attracted to him. He asked if he could take her to dinner and she agreed.

Ebony is a self-described "bougie" woman who enjoys fine dining and upscale experiences. She also has a down-to- earth side that allows her to have a beer at sports bar and loudly (and quite obnoxiously) root for her favorite football team. If you met Ebony in either one of these social settings, you'd be shocked if you saw her in the other.

The gentleman that asked Ebony out was more the sports bar type than he was five star dining. He took her to a family restaurant that doubled as a brewery and they had a great meal and good conversation.

For about two weeks, Ebony had been taken out on three dates and on each one the appropriate attire was never anything fancier than jeans. Feeling good about the connection she was making, Ebony decided to introduce her new beau to a few of her closest friends.

We all met at an upscale restaurant and the four of us eagerly awaited to meet the topic of all of Ebony's recent conversations. Ebony and her date finally arrived an hour after we agreed to meet. I could tell by the look on her face that some issue had caused their delay. Ebony wore a black cocktail dress and heels; her date wore jeans, casual loafers, and a t-shirt. Right away, I had a good idea of why Ebony had a sour look on her face.

Ebony's date looked incredibly uncomfortable throughout the whole meal. As cliché as it sounds, he struggled with the appropriate silverware selection and was embarrassed by the waiter selecting him to sample the bottle of wine we had purchased for the table. He was out of his element and it showed.

Now, I'm not sure if Ebony had warned her date about how the night would go, but I could see he was frustrated and a little embarrassed. I understood how he felt, but he allowed his frustration to turn into anger and directed that anger towards Ebony. He spoke to her in a curt and disrespectful manner that made everyone at the table uncomfortable.

Finally, the painful night ended and as I suspected, the courtship between Ebony and the man ended. He was probably a great guy, but he obviously wasn't great for Ebony.

Like a job interview, we know that first impressions are not lasting. This is why long courtships are so important. The longer you take to get to know someone, the more likely the person will show you his real self. It's almost impossible to keep up a façade forever.

What troubled me about this situation was that Ebony's female friends chastised her for ending the dating relationship with the man so quickly. A few women actually advised her to be more patient and to *teach* him how to behave in those situations so the next time he wouldn't be so uncomfortable.

I adamantly disagree! It wasn't the guy's discomfort or lack of situational etiquette that made Ebony's actions appropriate. It was his reaction that made him no longer a suitable candidate for her time and attention. His discomfort was understandable; his anger was unreasonable. If choosing the appropriate fork to eat his salad with caused that type of anger, then she could almost be assured that his temper would eventually become an issue.

Besides, there are far too many men in the world for you or any woman to feel the need to facilitate an etiquette class for the man you are dating.

Let Him See the Real You

Eventually, you should feel more comfortable showing the man you are dating the real you. You and all of your perfect imperfections should be displayed for this man to evaluate and decide if he wants to pursue a long term relationship with you.

He should do the same. I've read books on dating or heard advice that encourages a woman to engage in behavior that is inconsistent or completely contrary to her true identity.

This is such a waste of time and extremely misogynistic. A man should be given the opportunity to fall for the real you, not the person you created to appease him.

For instance, if you are the type of woman who likes to text or talk throughout the day, then text and call the man you're dating throughout the day. Don't limit your contact to once a day to make him feel more comfortable or out of fear that he won't like it. There's a way to respect his time without abandoning your needs. Ask him about his schedule so that you can find a less intrusive time to communicate with him. If you do play this game of pretend and modify your behavior in an attempt to not turn him off, eventually you will revert back to what you want. You can expect him to react to this change in your behavior, not because of your sudden desire for contact but your inconsistent actions. You see, there's a man (actually more than a few men) who may find your desire to reach out to him endearing and comforting. Why pretend for a man who doesn't share your values?

All the Good Men

It is a question asked by so many women; where are all the good men? The truth is that there are tons of good men, even great men out there. They just may not all be great for YOU!

The trick here is to reserve your time and energy for the *right* man who is *right* for you.

The only way to determine if the *good man* you met is *your* good man is to take your time to get to know the real him while allowing him to get to know the real you.

"Men" is a broad category and although we share many characteristics, men are not a monolith. It's counterproductive to apply a single mindset to all men. At times, you'll notice I'll refer to men as a group or I may even write, *some men*. All men are different, but there are patterns in behavior and repetitive qualities certain men share that should make it easy for a woman to recognize who she is dealing with. It is foolish to compare one man to the next, but when you are able to recognize the patterns and characteristics a man shares with someone who has hurt you in the past, you are better equipped to decide whether or not the new guy is worth your time and effort. As my mother often says, "there's nothing new under the sun." In other words, if Charles hurt you in the past and John is behaving a lot like Charles, get rid of John. He may not be Charles but he's close enough that you shouldn't waste your time.

It's easy for anyone to make broad, sweeping generalizations about men and women and it isn't until you attempt to apply that logic to one individual that you realize how unreliable those nonspecific characterizations are. The result is that you either miss out on a potentially great relationship, or you stay longer than you should have trying to force a square peg into a round hole.

Take the statements in this book and apply them to your dating life along with your powerful intuition, self appreciation, and discernment.

Allow the situations, illustrations, and stories I provide as tools to empower yourself to get exactly what you want out of dating.

Do You

Throughout the dating process, do you. Be yourself!

Don't change, modify, deviate, or limit who you are for the sake of a man. The way you are right at this moment is perfect for someone. You don't need to lose weight, you don't need a better job, you don't need to hide the fact that you have kids, and you don't need to adopt a set of rules that you don't find plausible to enjoy the company of a good man. Your appearance should be pleasing to you. The image that you see in the mirror should be a welcoming sight if you want anyone else to appreciate you. It incenses me that a woman is actually told that *she* is the reason she has not found Prince Charming. You are not the problem; the false and misleading persona of yourself you've created is what keeps you flustered in the dating world. You see, your mother was right, just be yourself.

You have to accept me for who I am.

Okay, I don't believe in this statement at all. I don't have to do anything and neither does anyone else. I have choice and free will. I don't have to accept anything about you I don't like. Furthermore, once two people enter a relationship, the process of evolution should begin for them both – collectively and individually. Changing with someone is very different than changing for someone.

Though this may seem contradicting, it really isn't. You see, the woman you present is the woman a man will fall in love with. Overtime, you will learn what traits you are willing to adopt or abandon now that you are a couple. Let me give you an example of what I mean:

I dated a woman who loved country music. Not the pop country that is played on the radio nowadays but the real, down home, southern-twang style of country music.

I do not like country music… any country music. However, I liked this woman. Despite her musical preference, I really enjoyed who she was as a person. I made my disdain for country music clear in the beginning and she accepted that I would never trade in my jazz records for cowboy boots. Over time, as we got to know each other and spent time together, I opened my mind and started to appreciate a few songs that she enjoyed. Music is a powerful medium of creativity and I respected her desire to listen to the music she enjoyed. Though we didn't work out as a couple, she broadened my horizons and I developed a love for the stories in the country music songs that she played. I didn't remain rigid and unyielding to the idea that I couldn't be introduced to something new. After I developed feelings for her, I didn't force her to take me as I am; instead I was open to evolve to become more compatible with the woman I chose.

Stick to your guns when it comes to those attributes that make you uniquely you; however, be open to change inconsequential traits that could help the two of you become a better fit for one another.

Fun

Ultimately, dating should be fun. The goal should be creating an environment that makes getting to know each other an enjoyable experience. You should have nothing but time invested while you're dating, so an easy, painless exit is always possible when necessary. Dating should never involve pressure or judgment. If you are feeling either, walk away.

Whatever happens between two consenting adults should be enjoyed by those two consenting adults. No one has the right to judge behavior or actions that you have engaged in of your own free will. There are no hard and fast rules to dating. You are the only plausible judge that can decide if an experience or a person is right for you.

No

No is the most liberating and powerful word in the dictionary. Not even *yes* has the virility and strength of *no*. Do not be afraid of the word and use it as a tool to gain the happiness you seek and the relationship you want. You have no obligation to let someone down easy or give someone a chance. Your preferences should be your guide. Your preferences belong to you and should only be modified at your behest. Don't be afraid to say no to anything. If a man punishes you for the word *no*, then he is not the man for you. A mature and caring man should be able to turn *no* into at least *maybe* without coercion or manipulation.

Settling vs. Compromise

When choosing a dating partner, you should never settle. You have certain criteria that you have in mind that a man should meet. Ensure that he meets each criterion.

Be realistic in your expectations and completely aware of what you want. Understand that certain traits and attributes come with a price.

When I was younger, many years ago, I purchased a Lexus GX470. I was so proud of that truck and proud of myself that I could afford to buy it. I could afford to buy it but I quickly discovered that I couldn't afford to own it. The maintenance on a luxury vehicle is extremely expensive and I was limited to where I could get repairs done because it was a foreign and luxury vehicle. You want a man who is extremely successful and wealthy and that's great.

However, be aware that wealthy and successful men usually become that way with long hours at work and very little leisure time.

You want a man who can spend lots of quality time with you. However, be aware that a man with a lot of time on his hands usually (not always) means he does not have a lot of residual income.

You want a man with a chiseled body. However, be aware that achieving the ideal body is an arduous and rigid endeavor with very little room for eating out and lots of time in the gym.

These are generalizations of course; however they are based on some truth. You may have to compromise on some of your preferences but only the ones of less importance to you. Only you can decide what those are.

A man can be a bit shy of six feet tall but be an excellent conversationalist. If you value height over conversation, this isn't a compromise you should make. Date only the men who fit your ideal. Low expectations may equal to broader choices, but it also means you'll have to kiss a lot of frogs to find your prince.

Patience

The folly of some of the women I've spoke to about dating is their impatience. They entertain men who never stood a chance and as a result become more and more jaded by the process. It can be difficult to be patient when it appears that others have found dating success before you.

Don't be swayed by what you see. All that shimmers is certainly not gold. Do you want to find a great guy or just an occupier of space and time until a great guy comes along? There's absolutely nothing wrong with you and you are doing nothing wrong. You and the perfect guy just haven't been introduced at the perfect time – but you will.

Your patience should be a result of your unyielding belief that you are worth the wait – his and yours. Don't be swayed by people who claim that you are too picky. You are not too picky!

Trust me, the perfect guy is waiting for you and the more time you spend enjoying your single status, the quicker he will appear. As a man, nothing is more attractive to me than a woman who knows exactly what she wants and who refuses to settle for anything less. See, if she's been waiting on a man like me, then when we find each other I know I've been chosen and not settled for. I'm not a consolation prize and neither are you!

Dating with a Purpose

Dating involves time and money. Regardless who pays, both of you are spending money and precious time. Little black dresses, makeup, babysitters, and other dating incidentals can get expensive quick. Do you really want to waste your precious resources on someone who is not worth it?

Neither time nor money should be used as bargaining chips to solicit sex or pressure you to engage in activity that you are not comfortable with including dinner, drinks, or coffee.

Know YOUR purpose for dating. Your purpose is the only purpose that matters. You don't have to date for marriage or date for a good time. You and only you can decide why you go out with the opposite sex. Knowing your purpose helps with the selection process.

You know not to waste time with someone who doesn't want what you want or who has a goal that is counterproductive to your own. Be upfront and honest about your purpose from the beginning.

I know a lot of relationships that started casually and became serious, but the intended purpose of courtship was well known from the beginning.

The dating process should begin with goal setting. Before you make yourself available, spend a little time setting realistic and achievable dating goals and then promise yourself that you won't change them for anyone... no, not even him.

Love Like You Have Never Been Hurt... but Date Like You Were Hurt Recently

Love is a destination that should be worth every step of the journey. It doesn't have to be an arduous journey but it should be a journey. Don't be so quick to fall in love... enjoy the fall. Enjoy the weightlessness and the descent into something wonderful. Keep your parachute on for heaven's sake! You earn no extra points for speed. Take your time and enjoy the process.

I believe in love at first sight; I really do... however, experience has taught me that my eyes can't always be trusted. My thoughts and feelings are much better at recognizing true love than my sight.

Have a high index of suspicion for anything that doesn't feel right. Be respectful to your gut feelings and the little hairs that standup on the back of your neck. Ask questions... lots of them! As a matter of fact, ask them twice.

Inconsistencies are a huge red flag and should not be overlooked or ignored. Honesty and communication are cornerstones for a successful relationship and it is not worth your time or effort to deal with a man who communicates dishonestly.

Be cautious when dating so that when you arrive at love, you can finally let your guard down. A close friend of mine, Stacey, told me that she has a difficult time tearing downs walls in the dating process. She says she is constantly waiting for the ball to drop. I told Stacey that being cautious is an excellent tactic and walls are what the dating process is for!

No man should try to scale or tear down your walls during the dating process. Instead, he should be providing you with the security and reassurance that YOU can remove those walls brick by brick. This is your process and if he values you then he will wait patiently. Be forewarned that walls are excellent defense mechanisms for keeping people out, but they also have an unintended consequence of making you a prisoner to your own fears. If a man presents himself in an honest and pleasing way, then take calculated risks at letting him get as close as your comfort level allows.

BE HONEST

I'm not afraid of my truth anymore and I will not omit pieces of me to make you comfortable – Ntozake Shange

It is often said that honesty is the best policy. This is truer than most people think. The most important honesty should be directed inwardly and not out. Lying to others has nowhere near the potential for damage than the lies we tell ourselves. Small, seemingly insignificant white lies become a mantra from which we live by and we soon wonder why we are so confused about what we want!

Be honest with yourself, first and foremost.

What Do You Want?

Only you have the power to answer this question. Often times after a relationship ends, you may attempt to convince yourself that you don't want to be in a relationship ever again.

I can remember, in my youth, enjoying a night or two of being incredibly disrespectful to my liver with a poisonous medley of alcohol only to wake up swearing that I would never drink again. Of course, I did. Now that age has decreased my tolerance level, I consider the consequences of each drink and I've learned the value of moderation.

I never really stayed true to my vows of never drinking again, but I did learn what I could and could not tolerate.

You should do the same with dating.

Don't lie to yourself about what you want or attempt to convince yourself you don't want something deep and meaningful because you experienced pain. Just learn from your mistakes and modify your behavior so that you can prepare yourself for an enjoyable experience without regret.

Do you want a relationship? Do you crave the familiarity and security of being with the same person every day? Do you constantly long for the *good part* where you are so comfortable with someone you don't feel a need to hide your true self behind the mask of your *best behavior*? If so, then maybe you do want a relationship. Pursue dating for the purpose of having a relationship with the knowledge you've attained from your previous experiences. Enter into the dating arena with honesty and the chances of getting hurt are significantly minimized.

My good friend Krystal dated a man for over a year. She fell in love with him and unfortunately the relationship ended. Afterwards, she swore off love and attempted to convince herself that she was just not created for long term relationships. Instead, she decided that she would just casually date and hook up with men she found appealing. All the while, the truth haunted her with every encounter she had with a man. Krystal's mouth said she didn't want anything serious, but her heart was attempting to turn every man she met into the *one*. As you can imagine, she fell deeper and deeper into sadness because she wasn't being true to herself. Once Krystal stopped lying to herself and dated for true reasons, she found a great guy that treats her well and absolutely adores her.

Does this mean rush into a relationship? Absolutely not! This only means that when you start dating someone or when you put yourself out there know that, like Krystal, you will have a propensity to want more. Armed with that honesty, you won't try to convince yourself that you can just casually date without falling for someone.

The reality is that many of us fall in love first with the idea of someone before we fall in love with the person. In other words, we fall in love with what the person represents. You meet a man who is successful and has all of the exterior trappings of the *perfect man* and it is easy to believe that he is the perfect man. However, when you get to know him you realize that he is far from perfect and as a matter of fact, his imperfections seem to dim the qualities that you found attractive in the first place!

Be Honest

If you are looking for something physical, then limit your relationship to one that is physical. Also, be well aware of the fact that physical relationships do not hold the same level of importance and are not viewed the same as emotional relationships. Don't lie to yourself by attempting to convince yourself that you are somehow above the stigma of a one- night stand because you *chose* to keep the relationship at this level. Leaving a relationship creates vulnerability and doubt that is not easily masked or hidden. The last thing you want is to be caught in a lie during a moment of vulnerability by attaching emotional feelings to something you claim is purely physical. Understand that a man's desires supersede any moral misgivings he may have about taking advantage of a vulnerable woman. Is this true of all men? No. Do you want to take that chance?

If you are not capable of dissecting emotions from sex then don't lie to yourself. Accept that your expectations of a physical relationship include some emotional maintenance. We love to simplify sexual relationships as something we do in the moment. However, understanding the biological differences between men and women truly makes the booty call an exercise in inevitability. It is inevitable that a woman will develop emotional feelings about a man she is having sex with unless that woman has been so deeply, emotionally traumatized or scarred that she is unable to. Some men understand this and use it to their advantage. Some men prey on women who are vulnerable because they are easy to manipulate.

Be Honest

Why do you like him? What is it about him that makes you think about him? If he looked different would you feel this way about him? If he spoke to you differently would you feel this way about him? If he didn't buy you things or take you places, would your feeling change? What is it about him?

These are very important questions to ask when dating. If you don't pinpoint the exact reasons for attraction, then you will find yourself deep in a relationship with someone and not know why. You should know why you chase a man. More importantly, you should know why you allow a man to catch you!

You should know so that if your feelings change, you can control the actions that follow. So many women get involved with men that they have idealized and can't understand why they stay in broken relationships. They build a man up based on perception and are shocked when the blinders are taken off. If you understand from the very beginning what attracts you to a certain man or all men for that matter, then you will be able to maintain a sense of control over your feelings about him and the relationship.

Be Honest

Be honest about your expectations and your standards; Do Not

Lower Them for anyone. If there are types of men you do not want to date then do not date those types of men. There is nothing wrong with having preferences.

Do not deviate from those preferences and expect to be happy. Do not deviate unless, after being honest with yourself, you discover that your expectations are unreasonable or unnecessary. Do you need "tall, dark and handsome" or would you be happy with "short, light and okay"? If you wouldn't be happy with a man that doesn't fit your criteria, then don't date men who do not fit your criteria. Don't venture away from that which makes you happy. Conversely, be honest about those criteria. Why does a man have to be tall? Why does a man have to be dark? What does handsome mean? Women are quick to dismiss a man because he isn't perfect and then complain that there are no good men. These same women will abandon all of their criteria just to prove that point.

Be honest. What do you want? This isn't the time to discuss or even think about needs. If a man does not satisfy your desires then your needs will never be met! If he doesn't touch you the right way, who cares how much he makes? If he doesn't speak to you the right way, who cares how tall he is? Don't lower your standards to find love. Adjust your standards after taking an honest assessment of what you can and cannot tolerate! Don't like men who smoke? Don't date a man who smokes. Don't lie to yourself and say "it's no big deal" to a character trait that has always been a deal breaker for you. Don't attempt to rationalize away his flaws.

"He drinks a lot but he's sweet when he's sober." No. No. No! If drinking is an issue then be real! It won't change. You will not change a man that doesn't have a desire to change!! If he presents himself as a broken man then you will not be able to fix him. You may be able to provide temporary repairs but you will not be able to fix him. Deal breakers are deal breakers for a reason!!

Be Honest

Finally, be honest about you. Don't present a broken version of yourself to the world and expect to find a man who has his stuff together. Opposites attract but not those types of opposites. The very qualities that you find attractive in a man are the same qualities a man will find attractive in you. Don't dumb yourself down for anyone! Don't apologize for your accomplishments or deflate your triumphs. A man should be able to stand behind, in front, and next to you. He should be comfortable no matter where he needs to be to compliment you, correct you, or celebrate you! If you lie to yourself and attempt to convince yourself that you don't need to shine then you never will! Every encounter with a man is an opportunity to teach him how to like you, how to love you, and how to treat you. If you teach a false lesson then you have no one to blame but you for the outcome!

Be honest about where you are in your life. Are you ready to date? Do you want to date? Can you emotionally handle the ebb and flow of dating? Are you searching for a companion or validation? Can you get what you need without dating? Why?

Don't get involved with someone who wants tomorrow if you don't have tomorrow to give him. Don't get involved with someone who only wants tonight if you are hoping he'll stick around for a lifetime of breakfasts. Men aren't stupid. Men are opportunistic by nature.

The structure of dating has taught some men to take advantage of any opportunity that presents itself.

You can't control the actions of any man but you can control your response – if you are honest with yourself. Ask yourself repeatedly – What do I want? What makes me happy? What are my boundaries? What are my deal breakers?

You owe it to yourself to walk into every dating encounter with a man with realistic, honest expectations. Otherwise, you will find yourself fighting with the lies you are telling him, the world, and yourself.

END OF CHAPTER HOMEWORK

As with anything worth doing, dating requires effort. Write down the criteria you want in a potentially dateable man. Create two lists. List one should be called "Husband Material" and list two should be call "Just Kicking It". In the first list, write down every single quality you want a man to have that you would marry. Be honest and be specific! What does your dream man do? What does he look like? What is his relationship with his family? Does he have kids? How old is he?

Now do the same with the second list. Write down the minimum criteria for a man you are in a non-committed relationship with. This can be anything from a booty call to someone you see occasionally without expectations of commitment. Again, be honest!

Now, compare the lists. What are the differences? What are the similarities? Are they drastically different? What does this say about the time you spend with one type of man over the other? Honestly assess why these men are so similar or different.

Next, assess your current dating life. Do the men in your life meet these criteria according to how you see them? Are you serious about a man who should be in the "Just Kicking It" category? Are you trying to make a booty call become something more than it is?

Finally, list the qualities that you bring to a person who fits the criteria of each list. What qualities do you provide a man who you deem is marriage material? What qualities do you provide a man who you're just kicking it with?

Which of these men do you really want? Why?

PRINCESS OR QUEEN?

I do not want a husband who honours me as a queen, if he does not love me as a woman. – Elizabeth I

Men tend to give their significant others a pet name. Two of the most common are princess and queen.

"She is my princess." "This is my queen."

Is there a difference between the two or is it simply vernacular or preference. Most women swoon at the idea of being treated like royalty and may make no distinction between the two terms of endearment. Many women probably long to be considered regal by the men they love. So it stands to reason that it does not matter if he considers you a princess or queen as long as he places you on a throne

Let's consider both titles and decide which is best suited for you. Are you a princess or a queen?

Princess

Within a monarchy, power is established and held by a single individual. All other power or influence is the byproduct of the monarch. For example, the king bestows his power upon whom he chooses and his lineage benefits from that power by association. It stands to reason that a princess would be one of the greatest benefactors in the kingdom of power because of the classic relationship that most fathers have with their daughters. The "daddy's little girl" concept is not new and stems from the relationship that kings had for their princesses. The women were exalted because the relationship could never change. The queen, though chosen, had to deal with the wandering nature of a powerful king but the king's daughter held a position close to her father's heart that could not be threatened by another woman – save the queen.

The fact that princesses were not traditionally poised to ascend to the throne without the aid of marriage was also a key factor in the treatment they received by their fathers. The queen was chosen, but the princess attained her father's love and prestige at birth.

From birth, princesses are trained to be a source of pleasure for their future husbands. The princess is taught to properly speak and act in a manner that would be fitting to sit adjacent to her future royal groom. Interestingly enough, the term princess was not commonly used for the daughters of kings. They were called "Lady" and were not considered a princess until they were married to a prince. This has changed through time but it illustrates the purpose of a female child born to a king. She would live a charmed and extravagant life but ultimately, she would be used as a political tool to gain power.

Queen

The queen is chosen by a king usually when he is still a prince being groomed for the throne. Upon being crowned king, his bride becomes a queen and reigns by his side for the length of their rule.

Though queens have served as the head of state at various times throughout history, the queen is usually the confidant and primary counsel of the king. There are countless instances where a queen's influence has driven the most powerful kings to war or even death. For this reason, even the most subservient queen's power is absolute.

Though she is confronted with the infidelity of a man of great power, the queen usually remains poised and understands that her place is at the right hand of her husband in spite of his misgivings. Not very many women are suited to be queen because they must be able to walk the line of holding power while remaining submissive. The queen must know her place while simultaneously imparting her influence into noble affairs.

Which are you?

In discussing the different roles of a princess and a queen, the major difference between the two is the lifestyle they lived and the role they each played. The princess is in a constant state of training and development; she is being prepared for greater things. She is lavished with gifts and adorned with royal favor, all the while she is well aware that her power is limited and only an extension of her father or the father of the prince she has married.

For the king, the princess is a temporary fixture in his life. She wasn't meant to be a part of his court forever. As a matter of fact, his eagerness to wed her to a powerful prince is motivated by his desire for more power.

Just as a king knows that he will eventually trade his princess for power, men today understand that the financial investments they make to modern day princesses will help them to gain status and possibly favor amongst other women. These men seek no counsel from their princess. The princess only needs to remain visually appealing and provide sexual favors as payment for their exalted, yet temporary status. Most princesses learn that there is a shelf-life for their worth. Just as a princess who does not marry by a certain age is considered an old maid, so is the modern day princess. Her power decreases as she ages because her beauty is the *only* means by which she gains favor. There are many women who never became queen because their focus was enjoying being a princess.

Today we see the princess in the form of the so-called "trophy wife." She is young and beautiful; although she holds favor with her husband, she has very little influence. Because she is not seen as a partner but proof of the man's prowess, her role will only last as long as the trappings of her outer beauty.

The queen, on the other hand, secures her place early on in a relationship. When a man refers to a woman as his queen he is in essence announcing that he sees her as an equal. He depends on her to sit at his right hand and serve as his primary counsel for life's greatest decisions. The unique nature of a queen is that her power is not limited to the power of her husband. Historically, queens such as Cleopatra, Marie Antoinette, and Nefertiti all exceeded both the power and influence of the men who brought them to their respective thrones. These women used their sensuality and intelligence as a means to command greatness and not merely as a currency to repay favor. The queen was not only physically beautiful; she brought with her a sense of her own identity, intellect, and influence.

The modern day king can be seen in countless examples of men who were pushed pass their own limitations by women who saw a greater purpose in them. These women do not require the spotlight and instead, prop their men up so that his ego is never threatened by her greatness. She whispers softly in the ear of her king in public so that his mistakes appear limited and his victories are abundant. The modern day queen does not see her place as subservient or support; she views herself as the foundation of her man's kingdom and so does he!

The man who recognizes that he has a queen provides more support to her than he does trinkets; he accepts more guidance than he gives gifts. He adorns her because he covets her. The man that calls his woman a queen recognizes that she is a long-term commitment and without her, his kingdom will fail. In many cases, a man will call a woman a queen well before he sees himself as a king. As a matter of fact, it is through her kingdom that he gains power.

Trapped in the Wrong Role

On some occasions, a queen will find herself trapped in the role of a princess. She suddenly becomes aware that she is not her man's confidant, but more so a showpiece to prove his virility. She finds herself drowning in his generosity but void of his gratitude. She is a queen adorned with the wrong crown.

How this does it happen?

Early in the relationship, many women enjoy the preparatory role of a princess. They enjoy the gifts, the attention, and the doting manner in which they are treated. Unless a woman recognizes the role she wants to play, she is easily duped into having an unbefitting crown placed lovingly on her head. A man will court his queen but he will also covet her ability to see his true potential. He will submit to her gentle correction and offer a respectful ear to her suggestions for improvement. Unfortunately, most women are searching for a man who is already adorned in regal robes not taking into consideration that a man appreciates not only the king he becomes but the woman who assisted him in reaching his royal throne.

A true queen knows her worth from the start and has a complete understanding of the power she possesses. She does not search for a man to complete her but one who compliments her nobility. Any pauper can be king with the right woman pushing him in the direction of his greatness. A true king does not shy away from what lies within him, nor does he curse the woman who attempts to pull it out. If a man fights your efforts to help him become better – he is no king. If a man would rather buy you a purse than empower you to fill it – you are not his queen.

The days of the monarchy are slowly passing. The new royalty of today is tied to fame and not lineage or pedigree. Every person has it within themselves to rule over their own personal kingdom. It is imperative that a woman knows her worth and never relinquish her crown to a man who is not worthy. Additionally, it is important that women understand the limitations of a princess and not seek a greater crown from a man who is not willing to share his kingdom. There's nothing wrong with being a princess if a woman is satisfied with limited power and no influence. However, if she wants to walk fully in her purpose she must be willing to help the right man find and achieve his.

Additionally, and this fact should not be overlooked, you do not need a king to be a queen. Queen Elizabeth II has been the Queen of England since 1952 and her husband Philip had no financial standings and was foreign born. You are a queen because you have decided to be a queen. You need no confirmation, justification, nor affirmation to sit upon your throne. Your royalty is based on the way you carry yourself and more importantly, the way you view yourself. Have the bold audacity to define yourself as a queen and then spend every moment of your life walking in your royal truth.

END OF CHAPTER HOMEWORK

Recall a time when you were dating someone that made you his princess or his queen.

Now contrast how you felt during each relationship (no matter how brief).

Create a list of reasons you feel qualified to be a queen.

DO NOT CREATE A LIST OF REASONS YOU ARE

UNQUALIFED! Every woman is qualified to be a queen.

Honestly decide at this point in your life whether you want to be a princess or a queen – be honest.

Now create a list of ways that you can help a man to become a king.

Finally, create a list of ways that you can recognize when a man does not have king potential.

HAPPY

The most common way people give up their power is by thinking they don't have any. — Alice Walker

Growing up in a matriarchal family, surrounded by women of all ages, I've learned the value of a happy woman. A happy woman brings joy and life to a family in a way that a happy man just can't. Women are largely social creatures and are able to create significant bonds fairly quickly. It's quite remarkable to go out to dinner with my friends and see tables of women actively engaging in conversation and bonding with one another. On the flip side, men are largely stunted in their ability to create bonds. Most men form superficial relationships over shared interests that rarely go further than a favorite sports team or hobby. This isn't a hard and fast rule by any means, but it is a stereotype that is steeped in observable evidence.

Some of the women in my family, as well as female friends have found themselves happily single. In speaking with these women, I've discovered that they have not reached a level of contentment with the idea of being single forever, but they are satisfied with being single for the moment. One cousin of mine informed me that she has reached a point of sublime happiness with herself that she previously never enjoyed. Although she seeks constant opportunities for self-improvement, socially, financially, emotionally, and physically; she is very happy with herself in every moment that passes. She looks in the mirror and is pleased with the queen who is staring back at her. As a matter of fact, she remarked that her dating prospects have increased since she has found so much admiration for herself.

This is no strange or even curious phenomenon. It is unlikely that a woman will find a satisfying and fulfilling courtship with a man if she is not happy with herself. She is now asking the man to do something that she isn't – to see value where she sees none.

Happiness seems like a simple concept but it eludes so many of us, especially as we get older. Like many of the pleasures we haphazardly enjoyed in our youth, happiness has become scarcer and more difficult to obtain. There was a time that I could eat anything I wanted without a care in the world of how the sugar and carbohydrates were being processed or stored in my body. At the beginning of the work week, I would exercise out of sheer joy and not the necessity to keep my waistline in check. Now, I'm conscious of every morsel that touches my lips. I count calories in the same manner that I count potential hours of sleep. At forty-one years old, every slice of cake, every hamburger, and piece of bread I consume is accompanied by pants-tightening consequences that are difficult to accept. Happiness is no different.

I wasn't bogged down by life in my youth. My teens and twenties were pretty carefree. I had responsibilities, but my approach to them was more lackadaisical because I had the benefit of time to make necessary adjustments. Even experiencing divorce in my late twenties didn't immediately feel like a life altering event. I accepted the loss and looked forward to a possible future with someone else. Things have certainly changed. My responsibilities have increased and have come with seemingly impossible deadlines and immense pressure. All of this is perceived, of course, but no less real. Being happy is the choice it has always been, but now it takes a little more of a concerted effort.

Let me be clear, happiness is a choice! You choose to be happy or you choose to be miserable. Despite what is going on around you, happiness does not have to elude you if you make the choice to be happy. To paraphrase the Apostle Paul in the Book of Acts, *I think myself happy!*

Happiness derived from an internal effort. It irritates me when I hear a woman proclaim, "He makes me happy." I understand the sentiment and the intent behind the statement, but the semantics causes my stomach to turn. No one, absolutely no one can make another person happy. It just doesn't happen that way. We have people in our lives that bring smiles to our faces or feelings of joy, but those people cannot create happiness. No, the only ability we possess when it comes to another person's happiness is facilitating an environment that happiness can exist uninterrupted.

He Will Not Make You Happy

If you have not reached a place where you can summon happiness at will, then no man – absolutely no man– will be able to create happiness inside of you. As a matter of fact, his attempts at making you happy will only result in a growing disdain for him. His insistence on you being in a joyous state will be a source of discontent that will not easily be overcome. Worse yet, you will grow to hate his ability to find happiness in situations that you see only sorrow and despair.

You Will Settle

The worse part about seeking happiness in another person is the tendency to settle for anything that resembles happiness. It's as simple as the difference between eating for pleasure and eating to satisfy hunger. I've spoken to women who have been in substandard or unsatisfying relationships and found that the common denominator was their belief that none of them felt they deserved a better man. Some even remarked that they had convinced themselves that being unhappy with someone was better than being alone. On the surface this makes no sense, but if we dig a bit deeper the thought process is actually quite logical. If I am the source of my unhappiness, I wouldn't want to be alone so that I'm forced to face the fact that I'm the cause of my sadness. I'd rather have someone, actually anyone else to blame.

Now when I speak of unhappiness, I don't necessarily mean depression or overt sadness. I'm not speaking of someone who may need professional intervention to deal with a mental illness or assistance in dealing with a traumatic event like death. No, I'm speaking of a general sense of feeling undeserving of pleasure. This can be a powerful feeling birthed by the sense of unworthiness or self-loathing. Social pressures don't help. Women are bombarded with images and subliminal messages that unfairly suggest unimportance or undervalue. Unrealistic and unachievable expectations are forced down a woman's throat constantly every time she turns on a television or logs on to a computer. Women are constantly questioned about their ability to be a great mother, great wife, or even a great woman. Even women who have achieved great power and wealth are lauded with so much negativity it causes them to hate their success. The end result is a woman modifying her standards or violating her ethics in search of a bit of happiness.

If you are experiencing this type of unhappiness, your single status is a gift! I strongly suggest that you use this season of being alone to seek opportunities to find your happiness. If I may be permitted to preach from my own soapbox for a moment, God wants you to be insanely happy! He wants you to free yourself of worry, guilt, and anxiety.

Philippians 4:6-7 - Be anxious for nothing, but in everything by prayer and supplication, with thanksgiving, let your requests be made known to God; and the peace of God, which surpasses all understanding, will guard your hearts and minds through Christ Jesus. (KJV)

Okay... I'm done... for now.

Let Me Be Great

I have a dear friend, Angela who loves to tease me with the phrase, "let me be great" whenever I offer my self- proclaimed idea of words of wisdom. As I stated, I have neither the credentials nor the history of success to offer anyone advice so Angela's teasing isn't without merit. She's right. She has the right to seek and achieve whatever greatness she desires. Ultimately, it is not my job to *shield* her from harm's way, because she is more than capable of being her own counsel. Whether she takes my advice is inconsequential; she has made it clear that she trusts herself above all others. Angela is her best ally and I would do well to respect the love and admiration that she has garnered for herself over the years. To question her decisions is to question the love she has for herself. My response to her is always, "be great" because that pursuit, in my humble and unqualified opinion, is hers alone to make.

The pursuit of individual greatness is the key to happiness. First, everyone needs to define greatness for themselves and then "be great" based on that definition. Greatness may not involve losing 20lbs but finding clothes that make the excess 20lbs look fabulous. Greatness may not be getting another promotion but pursuing a career change. Greatness may not be having another child but celebrating that your children are grown. Greatness could be traveling around the world, the state, or the other side of the city. Be great. Seek opportunities to be great every single day and when the day is ending, take inventory of your accomplishments, no matter how large or how small.

Be great. More importantly, ensure you surround yourself with people who allow you to be great without assistance, provocation, or admonishment. You don't need cheerleaders but you should have a few valued stockholders who have a vested interest in both your pursuit and achievement of greatness. Take only the advice that you choose to take and either file or toss the rest. Don't allow anyone else in the driver seat of your journey and don't share your destination with anyone who doesn't have the vision to celebrate every step.

Be great. Here's what I've discovered about happiness; there is an energy in happiness that is unavoidably attractive. You will find yourself surrounded by other happy and great people. They will uncontrollably flock to you and you will create a synergy that is undeniable. You will also find that you are quickly able to recognize people who are unhappy and discontent and you will be able to avoid those people at all cost.

Haters

I've always felt that haters are a necessity. Even if negativity doesn't motivate you, having a few naysayers around just reminds you that you are being productive. No one actively hates stagnation.

Having said that, "hating" in a relationship is a dangerous undertaking. No one can make you happy, but you can certainly be robbed of happiness. A happy person placed in a chaotic and miserable environment can quickly lose her joy. It seems to be a simple task to avoid this type of environment, but unfortunately, perpetually dissatisfied people are extremely good at hiding and can even mask their unhappiness, but not for long.

A simple way of ensuring you are not inviting a joy stealer in your life, even momentarily, is to be mindful of his reaction to your happiness.

Does he purposely ruin joyful moods with sarcasm or negativity?

Does he scoff at your triumphs and revel in your failures?

Does he poke holes in your dreams or offer very little enthusiasm for your plans?

Is anger his favorite emotion, even when it is inappropriate?

Is your greatness a source of his misery?

You cannot fix this person anymore than he can fix you. I have encountered so many female family members and friends who have wasted years of their lives and a large portion of their money trying to create happiness inside of a miserable person. It's a waste of time and resources. Even if you have developed strong and very real feelings and invested a significant amount of emotional equity into him, my unsolicited advice is to walk away. You will be left bitter and robbed not only of your happiness but any chance to create future happiness. Misery truly loves company and it is the unintended goal of the miserable to spread their sadness like a plague.

Being great does not mean being a fool. There are paths to happiness and each one is intrinsic and unaccompanied. Be wary of anyone who seeks to improve or upgrade you without your assistance. Be even more wary of anyone who makes you the source of their happiness. You are not. You are a very shallow solution to a very deep problem. The moments of laughter you provide in the beginning will soon be replaced with anger, sadness, and rage.

END OF CHAPTER HOMEWORK

Assess your level of happiness at this moment in your life. Make a list of all the things in your life currently that give you joy. This list should only include current possessions, accomplishments, goals, and relationships. Although "things" can't provide happiness, they do provide a sense of pleasure that can facilitate happiness.

Now make a separate list of what you can include or acquire in your life that will give you happiness. This list should include things you want but have not began to pursue. For instance, if you want to finish or return to school but you have not yet started or signed up. If you have started an education program, no matter what stage, then completing school will go on the previous list.

These lists are external stimulators that facilitate your happiness. Identifying these items, experiences, or relationships can quickly put you in a "happy place" when you need it most.

Think of a time in your life that you experienced the most joy. You don't have to be extremely specific, but try to narrow it down to a single experience, (i.e. the birth of a child, graduation, a first kiss, buying your first home, etc.). Be careful not to romanticize a particular experience by purposefully excluding the negative portions or minimizing them. Reminiscing on happy times can be a useful way to remind yourself that you can experience joy. Don't get stuck in that time though! This should be a temporary trip backwards, not dwelling on the past.

Assess your current relationships and ensure that everyone in your life facilitates opportunities for you to be happy. Try to remove or at the very least, create space between you and anyone who makes attempts to steal your joy. Limit your involvement with this person if they cannot be completely removed.

UNEQUALLY YOKED

Be ye not unequally yoked together with unbelievers: for what fellowship hath righteousness with unrighteousness? And what communion hath light with darkness? – 2 Corinthians 6:14, (KJV)

Most people will agree that there are three topics that you should avoid in mixed company: sex, politics, and religion. During the dating process, all three of these subjects should be discussed in great detail. You owe it to yourself to at least get a better understanding of who is sharing your time and possibly your bed.

The Bible, in 2 Corinthians 6:14, warns us not to allow ourselves to be unequally yoked together with unbelievers. Now I'm no biblical scholar, but I do understand the analogy. During the agrarian period, it was not uncommon to place two oxen in a yoke, a wooden crosspiece that fastens over the neck of two animals and attaches to a plow or cart they pull. The animals were yoked so that they could combine their individual strength and pull twice or even three times the load (think synergy). The animals had to be similar in size, weight, and age in order to be effective. Otherwise, the stronger of the two animals would have a higher labor burden because it would have to pull its share, the share of the weaker animal, AND the weaker animal. All things being equal, the animals share the burden and can even accommodate for one another throughout the duration of the task.

*Note: Being unequally yoked has nothing to do with eggs…

Marriage or even long term relationships can serve as a sort of yoke. Two people are connected together with a common goal. Each should give maximum effort in the areas of their strength to make the relationship enjoyable, productive, and worthwhile. Unlike a literal yoke, physical strength is not the primary quality; you can be strong in areas that your partner is weak and vice versa. However, if you are yoked with someone who doesn't share your values, goals, or ideology, you will soon find yourself pulling in the opposite direction of your mate and going absolutely nowhere and putting out a ton of effort while accomplishing nothing.

Politics

I actually know quite a few successful couples who are diametrically opposed politically and it works for them. The one characteristic they share is open communication. They allow themselves to disagree without injuring their partner's feelings or belittling their partner's opinions. It's tricky. Political views are steeped in passion and world events can inflame those passions. One news story can polarize a couple to the point of what feels exactly like war. You know yourself. You know how you feel about certain social, economic, and political issues better than anyone. You also know what you are able to open your mind to without experiencing frustration and anger. I caution you to enter carefully into a space that you know will cause confusion and mayhem. It isn't fun to be on opposite sides of an issue with someone whose company you really enjoy. It takes an enormous amount of maturity to allow someone to vehemently oppose you and then share an intimate moment.

Of course, there isn't much excitement in constantly preaching to the choir. I dated a woman once whose political views were staunchly different than mine. On a few issues we met in the middle but on others we were worlds apart. We attempted to agree to disagree on certain matters but in our world with information available at the push of an electronic button, it was hard to avoid certain topics. Despite the fact that we really enjoyed one another, the idea that we would cancel out each other's vote eventually caused us to go our separate ways. I've also dated a woman who had different views but she was pretty lukewarm when it came to politics. Her blasé attitude about politics made it easy for us to disagree without incident. The relationship ended but not because of politics. She allowed me to rant without interruption and although she didn't hold my beliefs, she didn't really care enough to allow opposite views to be an issue in our relationship. Ultimately, I learned that it wasn't our differences that matter; it was the level of passion we had about those differences.

Religion

Personally, I am a non-denominational Christian. I was raised Southern Baptist but over the years my belief system changed as I grew older and encountered different experiences. My religious preferences aside, when picking a partner, I want to ensure that if my religious beliefs are not shared they are at the very least respected.

I have spoken to women close to me who have abandoned their beliefs or worse, adopted a new belief system for the sole purpose of falling or being in love. This compromise of your principles, beliefs, and core values will be the first of many. You will find that you've lost yourself because of your willingness to abandon what should be the cornerstone of who you are as a person. You will eventually find yourself taking other drastic measures to please your love interest and one day realize you've totally changed into an unrecognizable person.

1 Peter 3:1 - Likewise, ye wives, be in subjection to your own husbands; that, if any obey not the word, they also may without the word be won by the conversation of the wives; (KJV)

I've spoken to women who convinced themselves that they had the power to turn a non-religious man into a church deacon. You have the ability to witness to the man you've chosen through your words and actions, however understand that his decision to seek a relationship with God is a personal decision. The above scripture is speaking to wives, not girlfriends and certainly not women who are dating. If you seek a man with a personal relationship with God, then the friend zone is a perfect place for the non-believer until he decides to receive God into his life.

Men have a variety of motivators. Some men will do anything for money and others will do anything for sex. *Anything* includes sitting on the front pew of a church every Sunday until a man gets what he wants. Spirituality is deeply personal. I'm not suggesting that you cannot introduce a man to your belief system or even that he won't eventually adopt it. However, in order for this spiritual awakening to be authentic, it must be organic and done for the right reasons. "I love her" is not a good reason to become a Buddhist, a Christian, a Muslim or even an atheist.

My grandmother was a deeply spiritual and religious woman. She was a fixture at her local church and served on many church boards and auxiliaries. She was an authority on the Bible and could quote every scripture from cover to cover. Her life and lifestyle was consistent with her beliefs.

My grandfather, on the other hand, believed in God but that's pretty much where it ended. I'm sure my grandmother would have loved for my grandfather to be as active in the church as she was but he wasn't and she seemed to accept it. A funny thing happened before they both passed away; my grandfather started accompanying my grandmother to church and would sit in the parking lot inside their car during the services. He loved listening to the radio, so he would sit in their car, smoking cigarettes, and listening to talk radio or sports. This went on for awhile. Soon he ventured into the church and started sitting on the back pew. My grandmother, being a church elder, had an unofficial assigned seat on the first pew. Over time, my grandfather would move closer and closer to my grandmother's seat until one day I remember them sitting side by side.

To my knowledge, my grandmother didn't press the issue. She allowed my grandfather to discover his own spirituality and he did. He never became as active as she was, but he did become a bit of a regular during church services. She may have motivated him or even asked him to visit the church but ultimately his involvement was based on his own desire and at his own speed.

I once dated a beautiful doctor that was funny and very affectionate. We hit it off quickly and thoroughly enjoyed each other's company. We did have a fundamental difference in our core beliefs but we decided that we wouldn't make it an issue. She was agnostic, meaning she didn't believe or disbelieve in God because she lacked empirical evidence of God's existence or nonexistence. Her scientific mind wouldn't allow her to adopt the concept of faith, believing in something as if it were. Things were great between us for about a year and a half, but as we grew closer together, religion became an issue. It was the seemingly benign situations that posed the biggest problems. Conversations at dinner parties became heated discussions.

Daydreaming about children became arguments about the necessity for christenings. It was an issue; an issue we just couldn't overcome.

Eventually, our different belief systems (along with other issues) forced us to concede that the relationship wouldn't work.

You have to be honest about what's important to you. No amount of love or lustful feelings will separate you from your core beliefs. You've been forming these beliefs over the course of your lifetime and quite honestly, no one is worth changing them. Whether you meditate, pray, or neither, your spirituality is very much a part of who you are as a person – it makes you unique!

Furthermore, if your beliefs assist you in formulating your priorities then you really should take the time and have the self importance to find someone who shares them with you.

Sex

I want to make this very clear; I do not believe that there is any magic formula that will accurately describe when or if it is the appropriate time to introduce sex into a relationship between two consenting adults. I firmly believe that the decision to have sex or remain abstinent is a personal decision that should be made by the two individuals involved in their relationship. Outside influences, no matter how well intended, should be accepted cautiously and sparingly. Whether you wait 90 days or 90 minutes is completely up to you! You should NOT be shamed or feel ashamed by your decision to have or not have sex.

1 Corinthians 7:8-9 - I say therefore to the unmarried and widows, it is good for them if they abide even as I. But if they cannot contain, let them marry: for it is better to marry than to burn. (KJV)

I would be remiss if I didn't mention the advantages of waiting to have sex for as long as possible. Waiting until marriage is a personal choice that truly has merit. When the Apostle Paul wrote about *burning* in the above scripture, he was speaking not of the eternal fires of hell but burning from lust. Sex is an amazing experience that has been horribly perverted in our society. The intimacy of sex has been overshadowed by the physical act. A healthy sex life should exist between two people who have experienced deep and meaningful intimacy between each other. There's a reason that in biblical times to *know* someone meant to have sex.

Ultimately, it is your body – I can't stress this enough. It is your body and your decision. Just be very aware that Newton's III Law applies to sexual encounters: for every action there truly is an equal and opposite reaction. Knowing the consequences of your actions is the only way to avoid being burned by those consequences.

When it comes to sex – communication should be the best aphrodisiac and honesty should be a close second. Rather than circling a date on a calendar, introduce sex by first introducing the topic of sex. If you aren't comfortable talking about sex with your partner, rest assured that you aren't ready to engage in the act.

Be honest with yourself. What do you truly want from the relationship between you and your partner? Sometimes we crave a purely physical connection. You must decide if sex is the appropriate method to have that connection.

Know that sex muddies the waters. Sex is truly a bell that you cannot un-ring. You can refrain from ringing it again, but what's done is done. Your motivation to have sex should be based purely on your desire to have sex. Your desire to have sex should be something you deeply understand if you want to avoid regret. Sex, for any other reason than desire, is an exercise (pun intended) in futility.

You will not keep a man with sex. You will not get a man with sex.

You will, however, attract a man who only wants sex. It is erroneous thinking to believe that *all* men *only* want sex. Let me be clear - MEN ARE NOT MOTIVATED BY SEX. Some men actually want an emotional connection as well as a physical one. I don't have statistical data to support this claim, but I would wager to say that most mature men are looking for something that lasts beyond the point of climax. It may not appear this way because of social distortions of truth, but the human condition is unisex.

The safe bet is to approach sex in a selfish way. Now, I'm not suggesting being selfish sexually but I am saying that the decision to have sex should be based on selfish reasons. Communicate your expectations and place your trust in a person that has proven to be trustworthy and you may be able to limit "buyer's remorse" when it comes to sexual partners.

Abstinence

Just as the decision to have sex is a personal one, so is the decision to refrain from sex. Communicate this decision early in your dating experiences and you can avoid the awkward conversation of attempting to convince someone you are worth the wait. You don't have a responsibility or an obligation to explain your desire to remain abstinent. You really don't even have to go into depth about the timeframe. A partner that respects your decision and honestly communicates his willingness to accept or reject your lifestyle choice is all you should really need or want.

You are worth the wait. You are worth the wait because you say so. Justification only weakens your argument; it doesn't improve it. If a man does not want to wait then he most likely won't. If he decides to have a sex life and you don't, then he's not the one; move on with the courage of your conviction. Don't for one second think that caving in or compromising your beliefs will end in anything productive or enjoyable. The art of negotiation is being aware of what is negotiable and what is not. Once you show that you're malleable on the things that are important to you then prepare to be a contortionist, because you will continue to be expected to bend on everything.

My desire, dear reader, is for you to understand unequivocally that you are in control. As I mentioned previously, *no* is a powerful tool. Any person you encounter that does not respect *no* should automatically be disqualified and be immediately removed from your dating pool.

As I taught my teenage son, anything that happens on the other side of *no* is illegal, when it comes to sex.

Promiscuity

I really hate this word. I hate it because although the dictionary uses an androgynous pronoun to define the word, it is almost always directed towards the sexual habits of women, not men. No one deserves the label "promiscuous" because there is no number of sexual partners that definitely defines a promiscuous person. Instead of worrying about the amount of sexual partners you have or had, it makes more sense to concentrate on the quality of and emotional impact of sexual encounters. If you can look yourself in the mirror and feel good about your sexual encounters, then you win. Again, no one has the right to shame anyone about sex.

My final thoughts on sex are from my own personal experiences; I'd like to share one man's ideas and perceptions of sex:

I will judge your desire to have sex without a commitment or an insistence that we get to know each other first. I may not have the right to judge you, but I will. I will assume that your eagerness to have sex with me is based purely on your eagerness to have sex. I think I'm a pretty good catch, but there's nothing about me that would suggest I have the power to create a burning, unquenchable desire in you to have sex with me right away. That isn't self loathing or self deprecation; it's reality. We may have had an amazing first date and passions may have arose in both of us, but your unwillingness to wait only communicates to me that you have a lustful desire in you that existed before I came along.

You see, I want to create the desire in you for me based on you getting to know the real me. I want you to crave every part of me; my flaws, my shortcomings, my dreams, my ambition, my humor, and every other characteristic that makes me uniquely me! That takes time. I don't want to be a placeholder for your sexual yearning.

Believe it or not, I'm not alone in my way of thinking. You see it is my male ego that makes it hard for me to jump in bed with just anyone. I want to be admired and showered with adoration because of who I am and not just because a woman needs a man to hold. I want to really believe that not any old man will do. Simply put, unsubstantiated sexual aggression from a woman is a huge turn off. I believe that sex is the physical manifestation of emotional feelings. Sex is a byproduct of love – not love.

Now if you find yourself either adamantly disagreeing with me or believing that I'm not telling the truth based on your previous experiences with men, then respectfully, maybe it's time for you to start experiencing a different type of man.

Sexual Confusion

On several occasions, more than one woman that I know has informed me that a sexually confused man has engaged in an emotional relationship with her while continuing to have sexual encounters with men. My personal views on sexuality aside; I find it detestable for a man to use a woman to hide his sexual desires for men.

I can't imagine the burden of coming out as a gay man. Though the world has become more tolerable of sexual preferences, there is still a huge stigma about being a gay man, especially in certain cultures. However, this doesn't justify forcing a woman to be involved in a lie.

I don't believe in the notion that you can "tell" someone is gay. Effeminate behavior is no more an indication of homosexuality than masculine behavior is a sign of heterosexuality. If a man goes out of his way to date women to hide is sexuality, I'm quite sure he has mastered the art of concealing any behavior that fits the gay stereotype. The only true indication that a man is gay is his desire to create sexual and emotional intimacy with men. So how do you know if a man you are dating is gay? There's no mystery here; you get to know him. You have conversations with him that reveal his desires, ambition, dreams, and fears. You pay attention to his behavior. Deception is deception, it doesn't matter what a man is attempting to conceal. Whether a man cheats with a woman or a man, his behavior is going to clue you in on his deception. Inconsistencies, periods of unexplained absences, and behavior that makes you feel uncomfortable as a woman are all good indicators that you are dealing with someone who has something to hide.

You aren't a beard. You aren't a tool that can be used to deceive the world into believing someone a lie. I know you may have developed very strong emotional feelings for this man but if his physical desires cannot be met by you, then you owe it to yourself to either walk away or honestly and safely redefine the relationship. You can be friends, but you will never truly be lovers. You must create boundaries; the same boundaries that exist in any other friendship you have with anyone else. YOU CAN'T CHANGE HIM.

If the man you are dealing with is fighting sexual urges for other men and has a desire to change, then this is endeavor he needs to pursue alone. You can't help him with this. He has to discover his truth on his own. If you decide to be a shoulder he can lean on or a safe place for his thoughts, please play that role honestly.

Yoked

Unlike the oxen, we have a choice concerning with whom we allow ourselves to be yoked. At anytime you feel the load is not equally shared or your partner is giving maximum effort for a different goal, you may free yourself. The dating process is designed to test compatibility in all things. Time is a valuable asset that is never returned when lost. Do not waste time or any other resource on someone that you know doesn't share, or at the very least, respect your beliefs, values, effort, and desires. You will not *change* anyone who doesn't desire change. If you ignore fundamental differences that create chaos, then all you will have is chaos. You are worth waiting for and more importantly, you are worth waiting for someone more compatible. This is more than a day's work; this is your life. Ensure your partner is an active and willing participant in your endeavor to be great!

END OF CHAPTER HOMEWORK

Consider your beliefs about politics, sex, and religion. Create a list of what is and is not open to compromise. Be HONEST!

Do not allow fear to influence your list. You WILL find someone who compliments you and respects your desires. However, you must first be clear about what you desire.

If you haven't already, immediately abandon any notion that your sex life, past or present, is tied to your worth. You may or may not need help with this particular task. If you find it too difficult to remove negative feelings about sex, seek professional assistance. Sex is a natural expression and a beautiful gift of humanity. Affirm that you will make sex a positive part of your dating life, whether you decide to have sex or abstain. Accept that it is your choice and no matter what you choose... it is the right choice!

BREADWINNER

Wealth is the ability to fully experience life. – *Henry David Thoreau*

In the late 1700's the straightforward colloquialism, *breadwinner* was coined to identify the person in a household who was able to *win* the most *bread* for a particular family. Bread was present in most meals because it was economical, filling, and fairly easy to make. The breadwinner was the person who literally provided the means for bread to be present on the family's table. The meaning has not really changed throughout the years. We still recognize the breadwinner as the person who is not only able to provide bread, but provide it more abundantly.

In a long-term relationship, identifying the breadwinner usually isn't an issue. As a matter of fact, most successful couples enter into a relationship having a very good understanding of each person's financial capabilities and liabilities. Preferences, expectations, and cultural norms will usually dictate an individual's tolerance for whom and how someone serves as the breadwinner.

But what about dating?

As men, we are taught early in life, even in the most progressive households, that working and providing are necessities of our particular gender and the cornerstone for survival as a human being. Even the Bible warns in 2 Thessalonians 3:10, *If a man will not work, he shall not eat.* Some will argue in commentary that the passage has a less literal meaning, but for the purposes of this illustration we will take the words as they are written.

Regardless of an individual's sex, an unwillingness to work should be seen as a red flag. Work comes in many forms and productivity should always be a favorable attribute. Whether that labor is in the home or in a corporate environment; or if work is performed for financial or emotional compensation, work is a necessary component of our existence and sense of fulfillment.

So what about the unequal accumulation of bread? Should a woman of means date a man who is not her financial equal? Honesty is key in deciding if it is possible to date or potentially love someone who doesn't earn the same wage. Many factors are involved with wage, so it shouldn't rest purely on a dollar amount. Earning potential, quality of work, type of work, and of course, the sustainability of work should all be a part of the inner discussion.

It's a touchy subject. Unfortunately, in America and most civilized nations, earnings are directly tied to education, skills, and abilities. I used the word education instead of knowledge because even a deep and profound knowledge in a trade will not supersede evidence of the knowledge in the form of a degree or certificate. Sadly, many highly degreed individuals in certain fields are not compensated according to the level of effort that was put into gaining their qualifications. As in the case of teachers, an expensive, advanced degree doesn't always translate into a higher wage.

So how do you make the decision if a man is right for you based on his earnings?

Simple; with an honest assessment of what you truly value in a relationship.

His earnings shouldn't be your concern as much as his earning potential and self-investment. A man who invests in himself should garner a certain edge over someone who hasn't. That doesn't necessarily mean that a man with letters behind his name and a plethora of credentials will be a better suitor. Just as higher degrees can be the sign of a thirst for knowledge, he could also be compensating for a character flaw that should serve as an immediate red flag. However, his willingness to improve himself should offer him the perception of a willingness to be *better*.

This concept shouldn't be limited to formal education. College campuses aren't the only learning environments. A man who has a trade and seeks opportunities to achieve mastery should also be seen as favorable. It denotes a desire to move forward. A man who is stagnant should be viewed in the same manner as stagnant water – proceed with caution.

"He's happy where he is and doesn't want a promotion?"

That's wonderful. Are you going to be happy where he is and the fact that he isn't seeking opportunities to improve his financial health? Again, I don't advocate equating wealth with quality. I believe anyone who buys the line that "more is always better" is basically a glutton. However, continuous improvement should be a valued asset. So he doesn't want any more money or responsibility; is he gaining more knowledge, skills, or abilities?

"I don't care how much he makes; I love him for who he is."

That's wonderful. Is it sustainable? Do you have expectations in a relationship that are beyond the superficial feelings you experience during the dating process? Are you looking for a provider? Do you require a man to fulfill a traditional gender role and sit at the head of your table? Will you allow him to occupy that seat if he is not bringing what you bring to the table? Again – honesty is the key in making this determination.

Good with Money

Money is a tool. Like any tool, it should be used the right way. You wouldn't try to hammer in a nail with a screwdriver; you could, but be prepared to be frustrated and unsuccessful.

A man's ability to manage his money wisely should be towards the top of your list of preferences. Even if he is rolling in cash, if a man is frivolous with his money, this can be a sign of immaturity that will manifest in other areas of his life.

Men should be responsible. Call it a generalization or a true character trait of manhood; you should value responsibility in a man. Men who are responsible with money aren't necessarily cheap. Cheap men aren't always responsible with their money! The key is to be aware when a man shows that he can use money as a tool to obtain the things he needs and wants, the experiences he desires, and the lifestyle that he has worked or sacrificed for.

Even a man that makes less than you can prove himself so financially savvy that he is able to stretch his dollars to a point that you are unable to guess his income. More importantly, you can tell a lot about a man by how he spends his money. Your bank account is a better judge of your character, morals, values, and priorities than anything else. By following the money, you can get a pretty accurate picture of what type of man you are dealing with.

Of course, you shouldn't expect a man to turn over his wallet and provide access to his personal accounts in an attempt to prove his worthiness. However, there are signs that can provide you hints to a man's financial health and awareness.

Most employed people are paid monthly or bimonthly, usually towards the first of the month and midmonth. If your dates are limited to the weekend after payday, then you might want to be a bit cautious. If a man is waiting for an influx of cash to take you out, then he may be living from paycheck to paycheck. If he is budgeting his dating life, then he should be able to spread the love around throughout the month.

Income tax season is from January to May. Be careful of men who get extravagant around this time of year. Again, you should desire a man who isn't frivolous with his money. Fun is an important part of dating but so is sustainability.

Be mindful of what he spends his money on. Men have been sold a lie that suggests flashy and shiny are the keys to getting a woman's attention. There is absolutely nothing wrong with luxury items, however those items shouldn't be favored over needs. Just be aware and keep your head on swivel.

I have a friend named Cathy who was dating a man that presented himself as someone who was very wealthy and well-established. He dressed nicely and took her to expensive restaurants and on very expensive but fun dates. Cathy was enjoying his time immensely but a curious phenomenon would take place periodically over the three months they were dating. He frequently changed his phone number. Over the course of around 90 days, she was given four phone numbers by this man. He claimed that he had a crazy ex-girlfriend who was stalking him, but that excuse never made sense to Cathy. She couldn't understand how the woman kept getting his new number.

Cathy also noticed on more than one occasion, the man would ignore multiple phone calls from toll free numbers. She felt bad about the feeling that she was snooping, but she felt it was odd.

Cathy asked what she should do and I suggested asking him to explain the inconsistencies with his reasons for the constantly changing phone numbers and why he kept getting toll free calls. Cathy, of course, felt like that information wasn't her business and decided that she wouldn't press. I insisted that she at least asked for clarification about the phones. I assured her that if the man liked her as much as she liked him, he would want to put her mind at ease.

With hesitation and a lot of trepidation, Cathy asked once again about the constantly changing phone numbers. Surprisingly (to her not me), he was honest. He informed her that he was having financial issues and he changed cell phones when he wasn't able to keep the previous phone activated. Now that Cathy knew the truth, she had a choice to make. She had to decide if the three months she invested was worth moving forward with the man. Obviously, his priorities were not in order. He had money, that was clear by the amount he spent on his clothing, his car, and their dates. However, the money wasn't going towards his bills.

Cathy decided that she liked the man and had a serious conversation with him. Without being condescending and respecting the fact that men tend to have large egos, Cathy suggested that they spend less on their dates and she would be willing to help him get his finances in order. The man was open-minded and accepted Cathy's help and to this day they are still a couple in a very happy long term relationship.

Understand that Cathy's results probably aren't typical. However, she made the right decision by relying on open communication to answer the questions she had about the man she is dating. Had she allow those questions to go unanswered, the relationship could have either ended abruptly or worse, she would have continued in the relationship with a sense of uneasiness. She took a big chance confronting her date, but in the end it paid off. What I want you to understand is that even if the man would have been resistant to Cathy's help or continued to lie about his changing phone number, Cathy would have had enough truth to make a decision that was best for her.

Potential

The concept of synergy is one that is often overlooked in the dating process. The dictionary defines synergy as the interaction of two or more agents to produce a combined effect greater than the sum of their separate effects. Often times, synergy is illustrated by the math equation: $1+1=3$. The concept being that the presence of "1" alone is amplified by the introduction of another "1", so much so that the result is a greater than the sum total. This is illustrated countless times in business when a great idea is matched with funding, business savvy, or contacts. The company, Apple wouldn't be a household name if it weren't for the synergistic combination of the imaginative Steve Jobs and the innovative Steve Wozniak.

Renovating vs. Decorating

The burden of looking at a man's potential instead of his presentation is often placed on women unfairly. Women are asked to imagine what a man can become despite the fact that he has displayed no proof of imagination.

If you have ever witnessed or have been a part of a house renovation, you know that it can be a difficult task that can exceed the original anticipated workload. As the work on the project begins, you discover issues with the home that you didn't expect. Foundation issues, termites, and leaky pipes can turn a quick renovation into a virtual money pit.

Redecorating on the other hand is pretty straightforward and simple. New colors on the walls, new furniture, and a few new drapes and suddenly you have a space that appears brand new without having to make any structural changes.

As you progress in the dating process, both you and your mate should start customizing one another so that you can both be a better fit for each other. At first glance, this may sound a bit invasive, but you've been doing this throughout your dating life. You've made small changes and so have the men you've dated. The extent of those changes is the issue.

You have to decide how much effort, time, and emotional investment you are willing to provide to customize a man for your likeness. Are you willing to do a full on renovation or would you rather a quick remodel.

He wears white gym socks with closed toe sandals –remodeling

He's never traveled out of the country but has a desire to.-remodeling

He is successful in his current job but has ambition for promotion or starting his own business – remodeling

He has anger issues and a very short fuse – renovation

He talks of dreams of being a CEO but doesn't have a high school degree or a plan – renovation

He refuses to stop contacting women he has had past intimate encounters with - renovation

Renovations are not impossible and when done correctly, can be very rewarding. However, renovations require an enormous amount of work and even more time.

Michelle Obama, the former first lady of the United States, is often lauded with praise because she saw potential in a recent Harvard Law graduate for whom she was an advisor. At the time he met his future wife, President Barack Obama was a young lawyer who drove a beat up car with a hole in the floor. It is said that she saw his potential and invested her time and energy in him and the result, of course, is her former address at 1600 Pennsylvania Avenue.

Let's be clear. President Obama's greatness wasn't just potential… it was inevitable based on his hard work, sacrifices, and achievements. He was the editor of the Harvard Law Review in law school and had already begun making a name for himself as a community organizer in Chicago. President Obama would have probably made it to his current position without First Lady Obama, but I have no doubt she played an intricate role in his success. Her involvement in his life may not have been the only key to unlock his success but it may have been the key to unlocking the front doors to the White House.

So how do you recognize a man with real potential? Has the man, who has been courting you, shown a willingness to improve his situation? Is he a dreamer that has no history of taking action? Does he make excuses for his lack of success? Has he repeatedly made poor decisions that have led him to a substandard life?

Do not invest your time, talents, or treasure into a man who has not invested anything into himself. You cannot pull greatness out of a man who does not recognize his own potential to be great or lacks the willingness to achieve greatness. It is a fruitless endeavor to build up a man who sees no value in himself.

The money issue doesn't have to be an issue at all. There are great men who are not threatened by a woman's superior education, position, prestige, or income. These men have reached a level of social maturity that prevents pride from being a limiting factor in their dating pool.

I have two very close personal friends who are married and have a significant difference in their incomes. Now I don't know the specific details of their financial lives, but I do know that the woman in this relationship is acutely aware of her husband's pride and protects it at all cost. In return, he is a doting husband who is quick to praise her and give her full credit for his significantly improved lifestyle. She strokes his ego and he showers her with adoration.

Essentially, a man who has trouble dating a more successful woman struggles with his own efforts in achieving personal success. He sees her success as an insult to his lack of success because he must now self reflect on his failure in chasing his own dreams.

Take caution with these men. These men will quickly turn into emotional burdens that attempt to rob you of your ability to enjoy the fruits of your labor. These men will sabotage your attempts at self-improvement and criticize your achievements, no matter how big or small. He is intimidated by you and angry at you because you achieved what he was too afraid to try for himself.

Money and Power

I've been told by women that attempts by men to impress them with expensive and over-the-top dates is usually more exhausting than attractive. The point of dating is to determine whether or not a person has the potential to be a long term or permanent partner – at least it should be. If a man is not able to show variety in his courtship then he may very well be rigid in a relationship. Be wary of the man that tries to make every date a *night to remember*. This opulence may or may not be sustainable, but more importantly it communicates an inability to just be comfortable. Let's be honest, when we envision *happily ever after* we are not fantasizing about a luxurious ball, night after continuous night. No, most people will say that they are at their most content in a pair of comfortable sweatpants, sitting on the couch watching television with someone they love.

Ask yourself; does he show he is capable of just having a good time without the lavishness, is he attempting to buy your affection or compensate for a kink in his armor that will eventually cause you to lose interest? Is he looking for gratitude or praise because he spends a ridiculous amount of money on you? Trust me, all of that gets old very quickly. Ask yourself, how will this translate into a long term relationship?

Men of great power and wealth are often hard to get along with because their fortune and influence often rob them of the opportunity of hearing the word *no*, a very important word in the English language. No is empowering because it forces us to consider alternatives. No teaches us that we can do without and provides us with the means to avoid painful consequences. A man can be wealthy and powerful, yet humble and pragmatic. Balance is the key.

Money should not create a power struggle in a relationship. No one should feel inferior or superior because of a lack or an abundance of wealth.

Each individual in a relationship owes it to themselves to take an honest assessment of the importance of money in a relationship. Do not be afraid of how you will be perceived. Money, education, and professional accomplishments are important, but they should also be realistic. A highly degreed and extremely intelligent teacher may not have accumulated a large amount of wealth. A talented high school dropout may have amassed more money than he can spend in three lifetimes. Ultimately, it isn't the money you'll spend together that will determine your compatibility; it is the quality of the time you invest in the relationship.

END OF CHAPTER HOMEWORK

Revisit the list you made for a potential suitor. Focus purely on education, employment, and income. Determine if they were a factor in the success or demise of those relationships.

Take a long and honest assessment of whether or not you can honestly date a person who has less education, employability, or income than you. Do not worry about social pressure or feelings of guilt in making this determination. Do not worry about what other people will think; other people are not going to be in the relationship with you. Ultimately, you will have to decide what is important or what can be disregarded as irrelevant.

Consider home ownership and other tangibles that you feel are a good indication of a potential suitor's desirability. If you didn't previously add these attributes, please do so now.

After creating the above list, number each attribute in order of importance from least to greatest. Evaluate the quality of past relationships based on those attributes.

THE TROUBLE WITH TIME TRAVEL

"I miss him for all the things he forgot to see in himself & if I'm lucky fate will help us rekindle a flame that never got set alight in the first place." –
Nikki Rowe

Invariably, every person who actively dates will stumble upon an old flame that either slowly fizzled to embers or was aggressively extinguished in an attempt to salvage a bit of self worth. Regardless, nostalgia has a way of striking the mind with temporary amnesia while simultaneously infusing the heart with longing and desire. Even painful lessons can be forgotten when we decide to selectively reminisce about past relationships.

I caution you strongly to be very careful when traveling back to an old relationship.

I can speak informatively on this subject because I've been guilty of turning back the hands of time on several relationships, including a failed marriage. It happens quite innocently. A text message, a phone call, or a post on social media is all it takes to allow the mind to wander into *happier* times. Scientists have found that the brain is very astute at suppressing painful memories in a vain attempt at self-preservation. We block certain events or painful experiences so that we do not have to relive them and suffer the trauma over and over again. This protective measure is effective until we find ourselves right back in the same situation.

A very good friend of mine made an excellent point regarding revisiting relationships. She claims that most people who revisit past love interests do not miss the person as much as the routine created with the individual. I agree with her whole heartedly. When reminiscing about a past relationship, if most of your fondest memories involve *doing* then it isn't the person you miss, it is the activities you engaged in that facilitated a sense of joy.

In your memories, be honest. Were moments of intense bliss followed by or preceded with moments of equally intense pain? Sure, you enjoyed how the two of you would sit and watch your favorite television shows for hours, but do you remember how he belittled you in front of your friends? I bet you miss how he would bring you your favorite foods in the middle of the night without complaining, but do you also remember fights he would pick when he had trouble communicating?

Now, I'm not suggesting that every revisited relationship comes with tumultuous moments, however those moments should not be insurmountable and illicit feelings of agony. If you can honestly say the bad outweighs the good, then it may not be worth the trouble.

Usually, these relationship "do-overs" follow a pattern. The first couple of weeks or months are usually intense and extremely satisfying. You spend most of your time engaging in the activity the two of you most enjoyed. Everything is going great until an old issue presents itself and suddenly you are violently thrust back into the situation that caused the demise of your relationship. You get mad at yourself. You knew better. You ask yourself how you could possibly make the same mistake twice. What's worse is you might actually beat yourself up over this relapse. Imagine punishing yourself or questioning your ability to be loved because you carelessly returned to a space you knew was toxic. Seems sort of ridiculous however, I've done this more than once.

So is all hope lost?

No, however, there should be some provisions that are made before settling into old habits.

Both Parties Must Admit Their Faults

I'm not speaking of who is at fault; no, I'm suggesting that each person admit the faults in their character that led to the relationship ending. We all have faults and not all of our faults are relationship enders. Some faults are inconsequential and benign. However, if you know that a character flaw or quirk created issues in the relationship, admit it.

When investigating accidents in certain industries, most companies employ a process that drills down to the root cause of the incident. Rather than focus on faults, companies focus on facts. Forward thinking companies do not want to just simply fire incompetent workers; they want to find out if the worker was actually incompetent and more importantly, if he was – why? Was it a training issue, a management failure, or procedure that needs to change?

The same can be accomplished in relationships. Instead of finding blame, it is more productive to establish the reasons a relationship broke down in the first place. Accept that either his or your attitude, expectations, or fears was the true cause of the relationship ending. Before you try again, ensure change has actually occurred.

Insist on Empirical Evidence of Change

"Baby, I'm sorry and I've changed."

These words have been uttered by so many daters

who are desperate for another chance to try again with an old love interest. Although he can sound extremely convincing, you owe it to yourself to view empirical evidence that change has occurred. Yes, he acknowledges that his anger was an insurmountable issue and he completely understands why you had to leave, but he promises it will be different. The question you need to ask is, "how can he be so sure?"

Has he dealt with his anger in a productive and proven manner? Has he enrolled in or completed an anger management program? Is he under the care of a mental health professional? Has he had a life changing event that induced a change in his behavior?

If you have no empirical evidence, then you are taking a huge risk. You have placed your trust in someone who has proven his ability to hurt you. You are not entering unchartered territory, but a well known danger zone and you should take precaution while insisting on seeing proof of change.

This goes for you as well! Consider your mindset when you were in the relationship. Where were you mentally and emotionally? Are you still there? More importantly, does he have the power to take you back to that place? We should all be moving forward and progressing in life. No one should be standing still and you certainly shouldn't feel like you're moving backwards.

Maybe he wasn't the problem; maybe if you are honest with yourself, you can admit that you were the cause of your relationship drama. So, before you go back into that familiar setting determine if you have changed enough to try again. You may find, after an honest assessment, the two of you are just better apart, and trust me that's really okay. Time may have healed your old wounds, but you are responsible for ensuring that you don't reinjure yourself with the weapons of convenience, nostalgia, and familiarity.

Maintain Autonomy

The easiest thing to give up when rehashing an old relationship is autonomy. It's easy to fall back into old habits and pick up where you left off. Don't. Your guard is down because he knows you and you know him. Lines become easier to cross and protective walls are reduced to rubble prematurely. Despite the fact that you know so much about one another, this redo should be treated like a new relationship. All the precautions you would take in a new relationship should be applied equally to this reattempt at love.

Remember, these are YOUR rules and they should not be violated unless YOU are comfortable violating them. If you wouldn't have sex on the first date with someone you just met, then don't have sex on the first date with your ex. You deserve to be actively pursued and courted in a manner that is consistent with your expectations. No special provisions should be made for nostalgia's sake. Make every attempt to make this next endeavor *feel* brand new. Otherwise, it is easy to fall back into old habits.

Do something new. Before you go back to old dating spots, try something new. Make him show you that he's interested in creating a new experience with you. Take it slow and enjoy the subtle dance of courtship. Don't be in a rush to get back to where you left off. If he is in a hurry to get back to a place of comfort, move on. He hasn't changed because he longs for the familiar. Remember the definition of insanity.

Rehashing an old love interest can be quite exciting. Familiarity can serve as a very strong aphrodisiac. You can avoid the awkward "getting to know each other" part but be fair warned that your ex is your ex for a reason. Something caused your relationship to end and if you have not taken the time to discover the root cause and apply corrective actions, you are doomed to repeat past mistakes. Tread lightly into the past and ensure both of you are given ample opportunity to display what you've learned from past mistakes.

Remember, you have options. Just because you loved a man in the past doesn't mean you have to be in a relationship with him in the future. If you truly miss the person's company, try a different type of relationship that has protective boundaries that will prevent you from experiencing past hurts.

Finally, you are not obligated in any shape, form, or fashion to try anything again. You should never allow yourself to be pressured into an experience that you previously didn't enjoy. Refusing to try again isn't weakness or an admission of guilt; it is simply a healthy desire to avoid the definition of insanity – doing the same thing over and over again, expecting a different result.

END OF CHAPTER HOMEWORK

Take a healthy, mental inventory of your past relationships. Note that some will immediately conjure up bad feelings. Avoid spending too much time contemplating those experiences, except the lessons you learned from them.

Are there improvements that you've made in yourself (for yourself) that may have caused the breakdown of those relationships?

How have you changed or matured since those relationships?

TIME & TIMING

To everything there is a season, and a time to every purpose under the heaven – Ecclesiastes 3:1, (KJV)

The origin and even presence of time has been a hotly debated topic in scientific and psychology circles for centuries. From Einstein's Theory of Relativity to noted psychologist, Gustav Theodor Fechner's work in the study of time perception, defining time has eluded man's grasp. We've learned to measure time and some have learned to respect it, but how is it defined? Is time linear or cyclical? Is there a start and finish or are we in an infinite loop? Are we living in a present that is based on past events in preparation for the future or are we stationary objects on an orbiting continuum awaiting old to become new? I will leave that debate for another book at another time.

For now, we will discuss time in a personal way. We will focus on the time you give to a potential suitor as well as the timing or moment in time you allow yourself to entertain a candidate for your heart.

Timing

I'll start with timing because if the timing is wrong, then it doesn't matter how much time you spend with someone, it won't work. So, what is the perfect timing for starting a new relationship or casually dating? How long after a breakup, divorce, or period of abstaining from dating should you wait before saying yes to someone's advance? Grab a highlighter because I've developed a fool proof mathematical formula that will tell you exactly how long to wait before dating again. Though not an algebraic equation, it will require a bit of thought. You'll have to factor in how long your last relationship lasted and the level of effort you put into the relationship. You'll have to consider your mindset while you consciously and purposefully remain single. Take all of that information into account and then simply ask yourself this question, "Am I ready?"

Are you ready for the possibility of finding someone? Are you ready to surrender your free time to someone who desires it? Are you ready to give of yourself in whatever quantities needed to develop a meaningful relationship freely? Are you ready to say *yes* to someone who may or may not be the one?

See, there is no scientific or psychological answer to the question of your dating readiness. Only you know the answer. Perfect timing is a myth. I'll prove it: think of the big decisions you've made in your life, or the decisions that life made for you. Whether those decisions ended in success or failure, I'm almost positive that they could have been made at much better time. I laugh when people tell me that they are waiting for a *better time* to make a decision. Very few decisions result in immediate action, so the act of making the decision rarely results in regret or failure. Deciding that you are ready to date doesn't necessarily mean you will be going on a first date tonight. It only means that you've made the decision to make your walls of protection accessible to someone you find interesting. The level of that accessibility is completely up to you.

Be realistic. Continuing the wall analogy, don't create a large, unlocked door and expect the perfect person to be the first to enter. Conversely, don't throw a rope over your large, impenetrable wall and expect your ideal mate is willing and able to climb over. Readiness still requires patience and caution.

Conflicting Messages

I recently met a very attractive, funny, and absolutely amazing woman named, Constance. We started dating and she informed me very early on that she wasn't ready for anything *serious*. Constance was adamant that she was interested in a long courtship and that she wanted a friendship that would eventually turn into a more intimate relationship. I appreciated her honesty and proceeded, all the while respecting her space. We went on about four dates, three were planned and one was an impromptu movie date that she initiated. We spent most of our time laughing and conversing about our shared political and sociological views. We were developing a pretty good friendship. Over the course of the month and a half that we dated, not one day went by that we didn't speak on the phone or at the very least, share pages and pages of text messages. Constance was the first person I either texted or received a text from in the morning and the last person I communicated with before going to bed. I was even introduced to a close girlfriend and then told the next day that I was given the girlfriend's "seal of approval". It appeared that things were progressing nicely.

One day, I made the mistake of honestly expressing my developing feelings for her. I complemented her beauty and personality without hyperbole. It seemed like a pretty benign, complimentary text. What I received in return was silence. In previous conversations, she warned me that her way of dealing with uncomfortable situations was avoidance. I sent a good morning text the next day and she replied with a good morning greeting. That gave me the impression that maybe she was previously busy or fell asleep. It was uncharacteristic but easily explained. I saw no reason to push the issue, so I replied to her reply by asking for confirmation that we would be keeping our plans to meet up that evening to celebrate her friend's birthday party. Constance told me that due to a busy day the following day, she would only be popping her head in at the party for a short time and she would rather go alone.

*Now I don't want to get ahead of myself and I'll go into great detail later in this chapter, but understand that a person will make time for anything or anyone they deem important.

The party wasn't exactly around the corner from where she lived, so knowing that Constance was still attending and denied me the opportunity to "pop in" with her assured me that the end was near. Not wanting to press the issue, I simply replied, "sounds good." I didn't hear from her the next day, as I knew I wouldn't; so I made the decision to bow out gracefully. A couple of days later, I sent a text message thanking Constance for the opportunity to get to know her but I didn't want to continue to pursue a dating relationship with her.

I wasn't sure if the text message about my growing feelings for her was the cause or just the proverbial straw that brought the camel to his knees. It may have very well been a culmination of words and actions on my part that led Constance to believe that I was attempting to advance the relationship beyond her comfort zone. Despite my efforts to avoid such actions, she obviously felt uncomfortable. She finally replied to my final text with a thank you and her revelation that she believed I wanted more than she could give at the time. Assuming that she was being completely honest, I was confused but I accepted her graceful goodbye nonetheless.

I was confused by her willingness and apparent eagerness to engage me so often if she wasn't ready to date with intention. It also seemed a bit dichotomous to introduce me to important people in her life if she wasn't ready for anything serious. Of course, she was well within her right to end our courtship and her explanation was a bonus and far from a necessity. Still, the confusion and rejection left in the wake of her hasty exit did sting a bit.

I did learn a valuable lesson from this encounter. Pace is subjective. As someone who despises running for exercise, I can say that determining the speed of a fast pace or slow pace is all based on the runner. The swiftness of a gazelle can seem almost sluggish when watching a hungry cheetah in hot pursuit. I honestly thought I was pacing myself, but it appears to her I was speeding.

Mixed Signals

I have a dear friend, Sarah, who couldn't wait to tell me that she found what she described as a "great guy". Sarah flooded her social media pages with photos of the gentleman and hashtags that would lead anyone to believe that she had found a candidate for the role of boyfriend. Sarah mentioned that she told her new beau about our friendship and that she was eager for us to meet. Geography prevented our introductions but I did get a friendship request on a popular social media app. As suddenly as he appeared in Sarah's selfies, the new guy vanished without a trace. I had to scroll quite a bit to see pictures of the two of them hanging out together on her timeline. Recent photos revealed his absence at dinner, concerts, and lounging by the pool – all places Sarah once proudly displayed him. Of course, I inquired about his whereabouts only to learn that he had been exiled from her life. His crime was confessing his love only three weeks into their relationship. Sarah saw this as a sign of weakness and desperation.

Usually, I concur; maybe in this situation I concur. However, it does stand to reason that this gentleman allowed himself to develop feelings that he misinterpreted as love. Though my loyalty remains with my friend, I do wonder if he deserves a small portion of benefit of doubt. If I was lauded with that much attention and affection from a woman, especially one as amazing as Sarah, I might mistake my lustful feelings as love, as well. Sarah presented this man to the world in a very visual way. Each picture displayed her affection for him and the hashtags suggested that he had already earned a special place in her heart. Giving my recent situation with Constance, I could be a bit more empathetic than normal.

Despite the fact that I was on the receiving end of an abrupt halt, I applaud both women in their decisive action to back away when feeling threatened. The threat does not have to be real. Your perception or discomfort is enough to walk away if you feel that is the appropriate action to take. Nothing is lost in the dating game but time. Whether I or my friend, Sarah's suitor was the perfect match is of no consequence. Something triggered an internal safety mechanism that both women chose to engage. That is their right and ultimately, their obligation.

Self preservation does come with one nasty little side effect – remaining single. As with any side effect, only you can determine your tolerance for the single life. It is counterproductive to proclaim that you want a relationship if your defense mechanism involves egress. There are alternatives. A simple conversation or pace check could prevent the loss of time spent with a viable candidate. If you decide that it isn't worth it, then by all means, let go. Spending time on someone you see no future with is time wasted.

The Loud Volume of Actions

If you find yourself constantly checking for emergency exits, it may be necessary to have an honest conversation about what it is you desire. If you truly are looking for friendship, then engage in friendly behavior. Allow your words and actions to be so harmonious that it is difficult to distinguish between the two. You are not responsible for anyone's perception or interpretation of your words or actions; however you should make an attempt to avoid contrasting behavior from your stated goals.

An easy way to determine if you are deviating from your desire to be "just friends" is to consider how you would feel engaging a friend in a similar way you've engaged a date. Think of a male friend you have and replace him with the guy you're dating, does the topic of your conversations or your actions with your suitor make you uncomfortable when applied to him? Then it is quite possible you've inadvertently crossed a line and confusion will follow. Be consistent. If you find yourself falling for someone, despite your effort to keep him at arm's length - be honest. Honestly admit that your feelings have betrayed your plans and allow him to make a decision whether or not he would like to continue at the pace you've set.

As you have a responsibility to yourself to not send mixed messages, you have an equal responsibility to not respond to them. I know men who have claimed that they don't want a serious relationship but engage in boyfriend behavior. One man in particular, claimed that he is only interested in casual dating but the women he dates are not aware of his lack of monogamy. Each one has been led to believe that she is the only candidate vying for his heart; however, competition abounds!

Boyfriend Behavior

Dana was presented with a similar situation recently and sought my counsel. She told me about a man she met who had previously gone through a very messy divorce. Understandably, he told Dana right away that he was only interested in purely casual dating. He made it very clear that he wasn't ready for a boyfriend/girlfriend situation. She was interested in him and despite the fact that she wanted more, Dana agreed to keep things casual and curb any expectations for a more serious connection. At the onset, the relationship was exactly what he claimed he wanted – a casual friendship. They went out to the movies, had dinner, and occasionally he would come by her house and watch television. He never missed an opportunity to reiterate to her that they were just friends and Dana reassured him that she was okay with that description of their relationship.

Then things began to change. He started behaving in a more familiar manner. He started to introduce intimacy, both physical and emotional into their relationship. He began behaving like a boyfriend. Dana found herself playing the role of girlfriend and she was happy with what she thought was the natural progression of their relationship. Though they never spoke about their advancement into a more profound union, she assumed his actions were consistent with someone who was ready for and desired more. As Dana allowed herself to become more attached and develop deeper feelings, he continued to display actions that made her more confident that they were becoming more serious.

Then the bottom fell out. Suddenly, without warning, he pulled back. Despite the fact that he had been marching forward in their relationship earnestly, he accused Dana of pushing him into something he wasn't ready for. Doused in confusion, she pointed to his actions and he diverted her attention to his words. He proclaimed, "I said I didn't want to be your boyfriend!"

Perplexed, Dana asked me what she should do about the situation. I advised her to give him what he said he wanted. If he wants to be friends then he needs to understand that friendship comes with certain boundaries. I told her to think of the situation like a menu. As he opens the menu of all you have to offer, he should discover two sides: a friendship side and a boyfriend side. Though he may be enticed by what's on the boyfriend side, it all comes with a price. The price is what she sets: monogamy, quality time, acts of kindness, and all of the other actions that are inherit to a relationship. If the price is too steep, then he needs to remain on the friendship side of the menu. I told Dana that you can't give something away and then charge for it later. You set the emotional value from the beginning. If he wants boyfriend benefits, then he has to be a boyfriend. If not, then he needs to behave like a friend.

Maybe he wasn't ready for all that a boyfriend entailed. That's fine, but he has to understand behavior inconsistent with his words only cause confusion and pain. My dear reader, no one is worth confusion or pain.

Time

I like the notion of *quality time*. It summons the idea that time is well spent if it has a certain quality. Anyone who has wasted time on a relationship that is going nowhere knows full well that quality time is always time well spent. Too often, we have a tendency to waste time with someone we know very early into dating isn't worth our time at all. We hold on to dying relationships for various reasons: we fear loneliness, we hope for change that is virtually impossible, or we are just bored. Here's the thing; whatever your reason for spending time with a lost cause, you will never get that time back... it's gone forever.

Your time is valuable. The value of your time is predicated on how you spend it. Even if you literally accomplish nothing and do nothing, that is still precious time because it belongs to you. Now if you can accept the notion that all of you time is valuable, then you can boldly be selective about who has access to your time. Guess what? That's your right!

I have a female friend who is currently dating a man that she is comfortable with but not excited about. Their relationship is lukewarm at best, and beyond the fact that they enjoy similar activities, there is no fire in the relationship. Quite often, she confides in me her desire to move on but two fears stop her:

1.   That he will somehow improve after their breakup and another woman will benefit from all of her efforts at attempting to make him a better man;

2.   That she will find no one to replace him.

These two irrational and irrelevant fears have caused her to mark time in a relationship that she knows in her heart has no future. Every day she grows a little older and a little more bitter, but not happy.

She will never get this time back. There's the old saying that, despite my research I can't attribute an author to: "you can make the man or you can take the man, but you can't take the man you make." The premise being that the time and effort invested in a man who doesn't want to change is wasted time. However, you can benefit from a man who has been improved by another woman's effort. Now, I'm not sure if that is absolutely true, however there is merit to the adage. Change is a result of internal desire and pressure from external forces. No one changes unless they want or need to change. So, if this man has shown no predilection for change while they are together, then he probably never will. As far as her second reason for wasting time, like anyone in her situation, my friend has to understand that being alone isn't a sentence or a punishment. Being alone is an opportunity for self reflection without the burden of attempting to meet another person's wants or needs.

During a difficult time in my life, my uncle gave me some words of wisdom that I've held tightly to. I had found myself in a lonely place. I had dipped into a bout of depression that caused me to become destructive. He told me, "just because you are lonely doesn't mean you are alone." Those words were life changing for me in that moment in time because he reminded me that my loneliness was a temporary situation that could easily be changed by reaching out to family and friends. I chose to isolate myself due to my loneliness and of course, my isolation created a situation that felt more desperate than it really was. I began seeking opportunities to fellowship with friends and family and suddenly, I craved alone time. I sought opportunities to just be in the company of myself to pray, meditate, and recharge. I suddenly valued my solitude.

I learned that I had to come to terms with my unhappiness and develop the courage to change my situation if I truly sought change. You see, complaining about the rain while refusing to take shelter is ridiculous.

Wasted or Well Spent

Time can either be wasted or well spent. When we reflect on moments in our lives that we spent time in a situation that didn't bring joy, we have a choice in how we frame those reflections. We can either view the time as a complete waste or we can conduct an honest critique of the situation and glean lessons learned.

After going through divorce my immediate reaction was shame. I truly felt like I wasn't marriage material and I would never find someone who was willing to overlook my past. I believed that I wore a scarlet letter that would never be removed. I made excuses for my failure at marriage in an attempt to avoid judgment. It wasn't until I took responsibility for the role I played that I recognized opportunities for improvement.

At my core, I still believe in the merit of a marriage union. I still have a desire to share my life with someone who I love and who is able to love me. However, I learned in the time I spent as a husband that more is required of me than just love. There are certain sacrifices that marriage requires that I didn't make in the past. I learned that the dating process is one that should focus on learning as much as I can about a future mate, rather than *just* having a good time. I also view marriage in a different light than I did in the past. By seeking the counsel of people in successful marriages, I learned that marriage has a purpose and married life should be lived in a purposeful way. I've made the decision to use this time as a single man to focus on myself and make myself a priority. I choose to make adjustments and improvements in my life, not for the purpose of meeting a woman but to be a better version of myself, for me. So, as I continue in my quest to be my greatest me, I look back on my past mistakes and pull from those experiences opportunities to develop good traits and remove bad ones. In all, I've learned that despite the fact that my marriage ended… it was time well spent.

END OF CHAPTER HOMEWORK

Make a list for all the reasons you are currently dating or considering dating. The list should include everything you want from the dating experience. Now honestly ask yourself if you are ready for each item on your list and if you are ready for everything as a whole.

Consider for a moment that you meet the man of your dreams tomorrow morning. He is perfect for you and everything you are looking for. Are you ready to date him? Why or why not?

Take inventory of how you spend your time. Sit and think about your work day or school day, now consider your last day off. How was your time spent? Is there anything you've been putting off because you didn't feel you had more time? Are there activities that bring you no or very little pleasure and productivity?

Carefully, think about past relationships (avoid spending too much emotionally energy on abusive relationships) what lessons have you learned about those experiences? What advice would you give a girlfriend that is going through a similar relationship as one you have experienced? Develop a plan to make the necessary adjustments in yourself so that you can avoid mistakes you've made or issues that were forced upon you.

CHEATING

"If you ain't cheating, you ain't trying!"

An old military friend would repeat this little mantra whenever we played cards. Rather than develop strategy, he spent most of the game employing trickery and deceit to gain an unfair advantage and win the game. Sometimes it worked. Sometimes he lost miserably. Luck played a small role in his victories in deception, but the most important factor was the person sitting across from him – his partner. If his partner was a willing participant in his illegal signals and poorly crafted code words, then the two would rake in books as if they could see each other's cards. However, when he played with someone who refused to join in his ruse, his lack of skill would cause him to make mistakes and lose the game.

Complicit

I've cheated in a past relationship. I allowed myself to be enticed by another woman and used the trust I had gained against the woman I was supposed to be committed to. I'd lie by telling falsehoods or by omitting just enough truth to appear plausible. Eventually and inevitably, I was caught. The paraphrasing of Luke's biblical warning, "what's done in the dark will come to light" is a truism that can't be stressed enough!

The hardest part of living a lie is the complexity in the effort to cover the lie. The truth is constant; it never changes because it actually happened. A lie on the other hand is fiction and not rooted in reality, therefore details are subject to embellishments and a very good memory. It finally occurred to me that honesty was just a simpler process and far more rewarding. I have made attempts to atone for my past actions, but the worst part about cheating is the damage that it causes is usually irreparable years later.

The question for a woman is how to refrain from being complicit in an adulterous relationship. A woman should ensure that she is not a willing participant in her own deception.

Let me be clear. It is never appropriate to blame the victim for being victimized. Despite your actions or attempts to protect yourself, you can still be hurt by someone who has a desire to hurt you. It's not your fault and you can't completely prevent it.

You can recognize early signs of deceptive behavior and make the decision to put space between you and a person with bad intentions.

I'm not proud of my past behavior, but I believe that change is a result of taking honest assessments of past actions and making a commitment to change. I made the decision to cheat but the ease of cheating was assisted by my partner. I wasn't accountable to her because she didn't insist on accountability. I hadn't reached the level where I did the right thing for purely the right reasons. I could blame my youth, my ignorance, and my selfishness; but ultimately, I cheated because I wanted to and because I could. Again, she didn't ask to be cheated on and she didn't deserve my infidelity.

Let me put it this way: When I was boy, about eight or nine, my mother bought me a chrome bicycle. I loved that bike because it gave me the freedom to leave my street and explore my neighborhood. I had a horrible habit of leaving it in the front yard overnight because I was too lazy or too absent minded to put it away in a secure place.

Eventually, I woke up one morning to find that my bike was stolen. My carelessness didn't cause my bike to be taken but it certainly assisted the thief in acquiring a new bicycle that didn't belong to him. I didn't deserve it, but I also didn't make any effort to stop it.

You have an obligation to avoid making yourself a willing victim. If a man wants to cheat, he will cheat; but that doesn't mean you have to assist him in his efforts. So, how do you know if a man is being dishonest? Simple, the dating process, if done with purpose, will provide you with your greatest asset in catching a cheater – routines.

People are creatures of habit. We develop routines and engage in redundant behavior; it's human nature. Most people wake up at the same time everyday and begin a series of actions that are performed subconsciously. Taking a shower, brushing your teeth, applying your makeup, and making your coffee are all as much a part of your day as going to work. Men are no different in the dating process. Men may perform certain actions later on in an attempt to impress a woman, but eventually a man will settle into a routine that is performed like clockwork. The time of day he sends a text message or calls, the days he meets you for lunch, the activities he plans when you're not with him are all a part of a well established routine that has very little deviation.

As soon as I abandoned my routine, had she been aware, she would have known something was wrong. I stopped coming home when I was supposed to. I cut conversations off in minutes that usually lasted hours. I stop making time for her and suddenly became increasingly busy. My routine had changed because I was developing new routines with a different woman.

Your intuition is a powerful tool you were given as a woman to discern between what is right and what is wrong. Most women profess that they "just knew" something was wrong well before they found out the truth about their man's indiscretions. There are a host of reasons why women I know have explained why they didn't trust their guts or act upon their intuitions. It's understandable that we want proof of bad behavior because proof empowers us to take action.

The dating process should alleviate the need for proof. You see, a man who cheats at anything usually will show a proclivity for cheating early on in the courtship. Wandering eyes, large blocks of unavailability, small seemingly insignificant lies, or even rushing the courtship are all signs of someone who may be fast and loose with the truth.

Wandering Eyes

It has been said that men are visual creatures. I won't debate the validity of that statement but I will denounce the statement as justification for a man who looks at other women when in the company of a woman he is dating. Self- control should be a key attribute that every woman desires in a man. If you can't hold his attention in a conversation, then I seriously doubt you will be able to hold it in a relationship. His eyes are telling you that he is still looking for other options. Even if it is your first date and you are open to the idea that he dates other women, you should demand he respect you enough to focus his gaze on the woman he is with.

Beyond the disrespect he is showing you by checking out another woman, take heed to what he is displaying as a priority. Ogling a complete stranger and being so transfixed on her physical appearance that he has lost sight of what should be his focus is a sure sign of immaturity and a man who lacks depth. You can rest assure that if he cannot keep his eyes fixed on you then he will have trouble with other parts of him straying as well.

Large Blocks of Unavailability

I like to consider myself a busy man. I have very little time to engage in any activity that does not bear some type of fruit. Be that as it may, I still make time for the people I deem are important to me. If you are a priority, then I will prioritize you in my day. "I was busy" is an excuse plain and simple, especially if it is given *after* breaking a date or days of silence. Our world is more connected than it has ever been in history. There are numerous ways to communicate, making silence a choice.

Unless you can state a specific reason for a man's sudden loss of availability, rest assure he is spending that time elsewhere. At the very least, you should have a high index of suspicion that should initiate a conversation. If you choose to just go with the notion that his free time is dwindling for no reason, then you are choosing to accept that you are no longer his priority. If you remember nothing from these pages, remember this - a man will prioritize anything that is a priority.

Insignificant Lies

If you lie you'll steal and if you steal, you'll kill.

My grandmother would assert this principle whenever she caught one of her grandchildren in a lie. She made no distinction between small lies and big lies. To my grandmother, a lie was a lie and every lie was the precursor to theft and murder.

Now, I'm not sure every liar will end up on death row but I can say with certainty that lying is a progressive act. You have to be cognizant of what you're being told and if it doesn't add up, stop attempting to force the equation. People routinely lie, will lie about absolutely anything. If you find that the man you are dating has a tendency to stretch the truth, eventually he will break it. It's inevitable. I'm not suggesting you end the courtship because of one lie, but you do have an obligation to make sure he understands that duplicity will not be tolerated in any form, small or large. There's no reason to lie in a mature dating relationship. If the man you are dating finds that he cannot communicate honestly with you, then he isn't a man worth your time or effort. If he lies in the beginning, rest assured he will continue to lie until the end. Save yourself a lot of heartache and unnecessary pain; either insist he remains as truthful as possible or simply walk away.

Rushing the Courtship

A courtship is a process that provides ample time and opportunity to allow two people to get to know one another. Each step in the courtship should be an opportunity to learn more about each other. So why would someone intentionally try to rush the process?

There are two possible reasons a man would attempt to rush to *love* during courtship.

1.   The impatient man is not in love with you, he's in love with love. He enjoys the excitement of a new relationship and is enamored by the intense feelings of falling in love and proclaiming love. It's been proven that certain pheromones and hormones are released during moments of passion and it could be that he just craves those feelings. Sadly, this type of *love* is rarely sustainable and fizzles out as quickly as it ignites.

2.   The eager gentleman could have something to hide.

The disclosure period of dating can be harmful to a man who feels he has some attribute, trait, or secret that he knows is a potential deal breaker. The goal is for you to fall head over heels for him and then find yourself impervious to whatever would have sent you packing if you had known about it earlier on in the relationship. If you set a nice and easy pace for the courtship and he is insisting on speeding things up, find out why he is rushing. If he can't articulate a reason to go warp speed then insist he slows down or make your exit before the inevitable crash!

When is Cheating... Not Cheating?

The idea of cheating is based on the concept of breaking the simple rules of monogamy. It makes sense that you have a conversation with someone you've decided to be monogamous with to ensure he is also onboard. Remember, what goes unsaid also goes unknown. It is reckless to believe that assumptions are an adequate form of communication when entering into a devoted relationship. Rather than assume you are going to be faithful to one another, declare it with words that are easily understood. State in simple terms your desire to see only him and for him to see only you. Simply put, if you haven't told him that you expect exclusivity, don't be shocked when you find out that you and he are not exclusive.

But what if he doesn't want to be monogamous?

Then you have a very simple decision to make, are you willing to share? Losing someone is not a valid reason to compromise your integrity or your values. If you feel sufficient time has passed and you are ready to focus only on him and you want him to focus only on you, then tell him. If he doesn't agree or doesn't want to stop seeing other women then walk away. Hopefully, you knew during the dating process what his feelings were on monogamy before you brought it up. Hopefully, you've made it clear by the second date your definition of dating.

So when is cheating not cheating? If it is mutually agreed that you are not in a monogamous relationship, then dating other people is not cheating.

Personally, I find it difficult to date more than one woman at a time. I don't have the resources or the attention span to spend time with two or more women the way I could with just one. However, if it is early in our dating experience, I don't expect a woman to drop other candidates in favor of me. I do make it clear early on that before I am willing to get physical or introduce her to the significant people in my life, I expect to be the only person she is dating. Her reaction and her thoughts on that notion will make it clear if I should even pursue getting to know her further.

Why Men Cheat?

I honestly hate this question. It assumes that the answer can somehow create a path to prevention.

Here's my profound answer to the question why men cheat:

Who cares?

My motivation for being unfaithful in a previous relationship was purely based on selfish desires, the availability of a willing partner to cheat with, and the naivety of a partner to cheat on. There was no cosmic reason that had my partner known would have stopped me in my tracks. The only thing that could stop me was me. Now she could have discovered my indiscretion early on if she had been paying attention, but she wasn't going to prevent me from doing what I decided that I wanted to do.

What's worse than the question *why* is the idea that you can "affair proof" a relationship by implementing some type of specific behavior? Please don't fall into the trap of thinking that you are responsible for a grown person's actions. You aren't. If a man has a desire to cheat, there is absolutely nothing you can do to stop him. You can make it difficult for him to cheat, but remember locks are for honest people. Instead of trying to look for solutions to stop or prevent a cheater from cheating, recognize his propensity for deception early on and keep him at arm's length.

I keep my man satisfied!

He will still cheat if he wants to cheat. He will have sex with you and then cheat; or he will cheat and then have sex with you.

My man knows what he has at home!

He will still cheat if he wants to cheat. The point of deceptive behavior is to not get caught. If he didn't value what he has at home he wouldn't try to hide the fact that he's cheating.

I watch my man like a hawk!

He will still cheat if he wants to cheat. You can't be everywhere all the time. If your man has a desire to cheat, he will cheat in whatever window you provide him, no matter how small.

I check his phone and know all of his friends!

He will still cheat if he wants to cheat. Never underestimate the creativity of a dishonest person. If you are with someone who has nothing to hide, then you won't feel the need to look for his hiding spots.

The desire to cheat has really nothing to do with you. I have friends who have cheated and most of them will say they truly loved the person they cheated on. They will also admit that a second chance without real change is just a second chance to cheat again

Once a Cheat Always a Cheat

Well, as an admitted cheater, I'm sure you can guess how I feel about this statement. I believe with the right motivation and the right assistance, anyone can change. However, there must be empirical evidence of this change. Personally, I took responsibility for my actions, atoned for my mistakes, and sought professional help to understand why I cheated in the first place. Through years of therapy and forgiving myself, I can honestly say that I no longer have a desire to cheat. As a matter of fact, I purposefully avoid opportunities to cheat in the same way a recovering alcoholic avoids opportunities to drink. I know how much insurmountable pain cheating causes and I never want anyone to experience that trauma by my hands again. So, I try to be both candid and cognizant. I am honest in my words and my actions. I consider how my actions will impact my partner. I make my intentions and desires clear from the beginning. Finally, when I'm in a committed relationship, I behave in a manner that is consistent with how I would behave if my partner was standing right next to me. If I wouldn't do it in front of her, I don't do it behind her back… but that's just me.

Dating after an Affair

Not everyone is a cheater and not everyone who has cheated will cheat again. I'm a firm believer that every single person is responsible for his or her own actions; however I also believe that people can be pushed into almost anything out of frustration. The Golden Rule reminds us to treat people the way you want to be treated. I think that's a great rule and would only add this caveat: treat people the way they have proven they deserve to be treated.

If a man shows sincerity, then accept his sincerity and return sincerity. Punishing every subsequent man for the actions of a man who previously hurt you will make dating a very difficult and empty experience. I don't know anyone who would be willing take punishment for a crime he did not commit. If you can't seem to find the ability to trust anyone, then maybe you aren't ready to date. Maybe you still need time to heal. When you are comfortable, be honest about your past experiences; you will find that there are men out there who are sensitive to the idea that you've been hurt. Explain that you have certain needs that must be met in order to allow yourself to trust again. Reward his behavior by rationing out your trust in small tolerable pieces.

My friend David was in this very situation. He met a wonderful woman whose company he thoroughly enjoyed but she had been cheated on repeatedly by her previous boyfriend. David's first thought was to walk away so he wouldn't get singed by the flames that still burned around her. Instead, he decided to have a conversation with her and simply ask, "What do you need from me to show you that I can be trusted?" This prompted her to provide David with a list of specific acts he could perform to gain her trust. He found that some of the items were negotiable and others were not. David made the decision that her list was tolerable and she was worth the extra effort. So, (despite our jeers) he performed the necessary tasks to gain her trust. When we would go out for guy's night, he would call when we arrived at our predetermined location and send her a "ping" through an app on his phone that marked his exact location. If we changed plans, David would call her beforehand and let her know he wouldn't be where he previously told her that he would. He made it clear that he didn't want to ask her *permission* to go out with his friends, but he was willing to inform her of his whereabouts. As the relationship flourished, he eventually shared his social media passwords with her and allowed her to check his phone as often as she saw fit. Eventually, none of that was necessary because she never found evidence of deception. Eventually, she just trusted David without the necessity of proof.

Now some might scoff at this and say it's "too much". Quite honestly, some of us, his friends, were shocked at how far he was willing to go to prove his loyalty. However, for their relationship it was appropriate. David valued her company and was willing to pay the price to earn her fidelity. In my opinion, it wasn't that she didn't find anything that won David her trust; it was that he was willing to work for her trust on her terms.

Communication is truly king when it comes to dating. If you think it, say it. Make it known from the jump about your feelings about infidelity and how you define it. Maybe you define cheating as communicating with another woman via social media or on the phone. Maybe cheating is any physical contact including holding hands and kissing. Maybe you believe the Clinton Rule that a man hasn't cheated until sex with another woman has occurred. The only definition of cheating that matters is your definition. You owe it to the man you are dating to inform him of that definition right out the gate, maybe not on the first date but definitely on the second or third one. Don't assume that it's common knowledge or that knowing what constitutes cheating is common sense. I learned very quickly in my military career that common sense is not a common virtue. So open your mouth and remove all doubt!

END OF CHAPTER HOMEWORK

Have you ever cheated or been cheated on? Take an inventory of the red flags that you were able to recognize in hindsight.

Make an honest and reasonable list of demands you will need from a potential suitor to feel comfortable trusting him. Decide if you are willing to ask a man to perform specific acts or if you are in a place that will allow his unsolicited actions to prove his honesty.

In your next relationship, take note of your mate's routines. Be aware of the consistent and inconsistent behaviors. Make a commitment to yourself that you will discuss inconsistencies in a non-confrontational and rational manner.

If you have experienced cheating, take an honest assessment of whether or not you are ready to trust again and make a concerted effort to deal with your past before starting a future with someone new.

COMMUNICATION

Who's on first? – Abbot and Costello

If you've ever heard this famous Abbot and Costello routine, or even the many reprisals of it over the years (the one featuring Morris Day in the movie, Purple Rain is one of my favorites) then you have witnessed a very simple illustration of how difficult communication can be.

Throughout this text, I've placed a fair amount of emphasis on the role of communication in dating. However, I haven't gone into detail about what good communication actually is or what it consists of. So, I'd like to spend a little time defining communication and providing a roadmap for improving your communication skills. Most of all, I'd like for you to be keenly aware of when communication is the reason for a failed dating experience.

Communication

Communication is a simple but often difficult process that is centered on a message. The message is truly the cornerstone of communication. The sender sends the message and the receiver receives the message. Both are individually and collectively responsible for ensuring that the message is sent and received with as little distortion as possible. That's usually where the confusion is introduced to the process.

Types of Communication

Before we dive too deep into improving communication skills, let's briefly explore the different types of communication. Essentially, there are only two: verbal and nonverbal. Simply put, verbal communication is what the sender says or writes and what the receiver hears or reads. Any communication that doesn't involve words or images is nonverbal communication. The crinkle of a nose, the raising of eyebrows or the motion of hands can all be messages that are sent and received intentionally or unintentionally.

Now let's be clear, you are not responsible for the interpretation of the messages you send, however you should take responsibility for ensuring that your message's intent is not convoluted due to carelessness. Often times, the message doesn't cause any issues; it is the manner in which it's sent. In this instance, the packaging ruins the package. I'm sure you've been on the receiving end of words that made a negative impact despite the fact that the sender swore he or she had innocent intentions. I'm sure you've even told someone at some point, "It wasn't what you said but the way you said it." A haphazard delivery can destroy a message or worse completely change the content of the message for the receiver.

A Good Message

So what are the necessary ingredients for a good message? A message requires three elements for it to have value to the receiver. The message must be:

- Clear

- Concise

- Correct

Again, we are talking about the message itself, not the delivery. Whether you write a letter, send a text, give a hand signal, or whisper sweet nothings; each of the above elements must be present if you want the message to be received with the intent that it was sent.

Clear

A clear message is crafted in a format that is easily understood by the receiver. Imagine taking Spanish language lessons from a German speaking teacher when the only language you speak is English. Learning in that environment can prove to be quite a difficult task. Now it's been claimed that women are from one planet in the universe and men are from a totally different one; I'm not sure of the interplanetary differences between the sexes, but I do not we all have a preferred way we receive and process information. I'm not suggesting you speak only the language of the opposite sex, nor do I believe you should be fluent in "manspeak". I do think it is advantageous to find a way to make yourself heard so that the impact of your message matches the intent. You may have to be creative or you may have to wait for someone who is willing to be patient and make every attempt to understand you.

Concise

I will never be an advocate of suggesting a woman should "keep it short" to ensure her message is understood by a man. Again, you will never hear me suggest a woman does anything but be herself for the purpose of dating. Just understand that long, drawn out messages are hard to understand and even harder to pull useable information from. It's easy for anyone, male or female, to become overwhelmed with a long diatribe. I personally don't even like long voicemails. "Hey, it's Tony; call me back" is an efficient and sufficient message to ensure the person I called knows who I am and what my expectations are. Sometimes, an economy of words is not so easy. Sometimes it's necessary to be verbose to ensure your message is both received and understood. So how do you know when to truncate your message? Simple, you know the receiver. The receiver will give you verbal and nonverbal clues that will help you to know when you can be descriptive and when you need to just get to the point.

In the same vein, you have the right to suggest a message needs to be a little more precise for you to understand it. Don't lose or surrender your voice. Be wary of a long setup and even more suspicious of someone who is constantly beating around the bush. Remember the details of the truth don't change and embellishments are unnecessary because whatever happened actually happened. There's a huge difference between memories and make believe. The truth can usually be found in the details and deception is easily discovered by the details constantly changing.

Correct

Honesty in communication should always be considered a best practice. We've discussed how honesty can be used as a weapon, so be careful. The message should be honest and correct but so should the behavior. Don't be so quick to reward honesty that you lose sight of the action that he was honest about.

Dishonesty destroys the communication process because the receiver is forced to provide feedback on what was communicated and that can be far from what has actually happened, is happening or will happen.

Consider, if you will, the Hale-Bop comet cult, Heaven's Gate from the 90's. A group of people were convinced by a charismatic leader that the Hale-Bopp comet was being followed by an extra-terrestrial spacecraft that would help his followers to escape a dying Earth. In order to board the spacecraft, the group would have to commit suicide and shed their earthly forms. Now, in hindsight, that sounds ridiculous. Everyone not involved looked at the group with disbelief but the thirty nine people who took their own lives in California believed their leader and took action. I'm not condoning or even providing credence to the event, but before we shake our heads and pass judgment, we should take a moment to consider the whoppers we've put our faith, time, and money into over the years. We may not have drunk the proverbial Kool-Aid for intergalactic travel, but I can almost guarantee that you or someone you know has been strung along on a lie that is just as silly. The moral of the story is that before you take action, ensure the message is correct and the messenger trustworthy.

The Decline of Communication

The most detrimental factor that has eroded communication is not the differences between men and women, but the fast- paced, one hundred and forty character, limited way in which we now communicate. I can remember a time when a well- crafted letter was the most anticipated form of communication for both the writer and the reader. We even had a special way we folded the letter so that its contents were preserved for only the eyes of its intended reader. Then, there was the triumph a man felt when a woman agreed to provide him with her phone number. Even the woman was filled with excitement at the thought that soon she would be able to spend hours on the phone enjoying conversations that involved only her and the man that sparked her interest. As a man, I can say that an enormous amount of thought and effort was put into that first phone call. Before cell phones, it was necessary to carefully consider the introduction, the artful evasion of a mother or father, and finally the right words to keep the woman on the phone for as long as possible. Any man older than thirty-five knows that the only thing more important than getting a woman's number and making the inaugural call was receiving her permission to call again as often as he would like.

Now, phone calls are almost considered intrusive. "Good evening, may I speak to Crystal?" has been replaced with "What's up, Girl?" Texting has become preferred over phone conversations and even text messages are now forced to be shortened and curtailed in order to be well-received. I was actually informed by a close female friend that she's a little freaked out when a man sends a long text message. The same woman also told me that an unsolicited phone call without a preceding text felt like an invasion of her privacy. Another woman told me that she felt violated when a man called her using a video app without first obtaining permission.

The rules of communication have change drastically. Dating etiquette has been forced to comply with those evolving rules and the courting process has suffered in my opinion. It feels like we've gone out of our way to put as much space between each other as possible. I've used online dating websites and found that there's a science to determining when to suggest a conversation is ready to leave the virtual world and enter the real world. Some women are actually more comfortable using their username than providing even a nickname that reveals their true identity. Trust me; I completely understand the need for caution. There are some pretty strange people in the world with very bad intentions, however getting to know someone with a firewall between the two of you is probably one of the reasons dating has become so difficult.

So what is the answer? Simply put, you must exploit the communication process for all it's worth. Use caution and go slow, but use the dating period as a method to truly get to know someone. Ask meaningful questions that provide insight and be mindful of the responses. There's no reason to spend time communicating with someone who doesn't speak your language. Personally, I hate so-called "text-speech" and I have very little tolerance for someone who abbreviates short words. In my estimation, it takes no less effort to spell out the word "you" than it does to just use the 21st letter of the alphabet.

But that's me. Some people find that method of communication endearing. The key is to not expect a three page letter from someone who favors "hbu" over "how about you?" and vice versa. If you find yourself getting to know a serial texter and you prefer phone conversations, let your desires be known and allow him the opportunity to either comply or show his unwillingness to pick up the phone and call. In the illustrious words of Maya Angelou, "when someone shows you who they are the first time, believe them." You will never turn a man of few words into a great orator; just as you will not be able to silence someone who tends to be verbose.

By all means, whatever form of communication you prefer, communicate! Speak your truth and insist that he speaks his. Be aware of inconsistencies and make the decision whether or not you want to put effort into discovering the truth or if it is even worth your time.

An analogy that is often used for dating is the process for attaining employment. The approach, whether it is by computer, association, or a cold greeting in a grocery store is essentially your opportunity to review his resume. Like a resume, you should focus on presentation and effort. I served as an interviewer in corporate America and found that a sloppy resume was a good indicator of a sloppy employee. A candidate who didn't take the time to craft his or her resume for the desired job would probably put the same minimal effort in their work. When a man approaches you, he displaying his qualifications as a potential suitor for you! You have the power to review those qualifications and determine whether or not he will be a good fit. Consider your preferences; is he the right height, and build? Does his style of dress provide an indication of the type of man you like? Does he speak in a manner that is consistent with how you want to be spoken to? Does he present himself like a man that you would enjoy spending time with? Remember, it's just a resume and a resume is used to get the interview.

The interview is your opportunity to begin the vetting process. While conducting interviews, I've found that some people will include information on their resume that is quite impressive, but patently false or a distortion of the truth. You find out if the candidate matches the resume by asking questions. The questions should be specific to gain the information you want. Be specific. Make sure he is actually qualified and if he presents anything that disqualifies himself, move on; you've lost nothing. For instance, instead of asking "are you seeing someone?" ask "are you dating anyone seriously right now". The difference prevents the opportunity for him to lie by omission. This isn't the time to compromise. He hasn't done or said anything that makes him so unique that you have to abandon your preferences for him. If you don't want to date a man with kids, ask if he has kids. If the answer is yes, then be honest about your desires and move on.

The interview process can and should last as long as you would like for it to. Information is power and this is your time to empower yourself; fact-check everything. You don't have to expect deception but you should have a high index of suspicion for anything that doesn't feel like the truth. Not only should you interview but you should welcome his questions as well. I've dismissed potential job candidates because when asked, "Do you have any questions?" they replied, "No." A lack of questions denotes a lack of interest. Remember you both are determining whether or not you are good fit for one another. You definitely should not be doing all the work. If you are asked a question, be honest. Give him the best information you can to arm him with everything he needs to make a good decision. However, be careful. This is not the time to unload all of your baggage. This is a date, not a counseling session. Just like in a court of law, anything you say can be used against you at a later date. Don't give anyone the ammunition to manipulate you.

A long dating process with effective communication should reveal enough about a person to allow you to make an informed decision about whether or not he is worth your precious time. If you "hire on sight" then you are going to get whatever you get. This, of course, is no guarantee. I've been on hiring boards where we interviewed people who are amazing interviewees but horrible workers. Be careful of the charismatic talker that lacks substance. This is why being your true self is so vital. Remaining in your truth will either force the truth out of him or have him running for the hills. Either way, you know what you're dealing with and you act accordingly.

Game

I was contemplating where exactly I should put the subject of "game" in this book and I think communication is an excellent place. Game is simply manipulation and men who employ these tactics are master manipulators. The essence of game is to find out what a woman wants and become it. You know why game is so effective? Because you provide all the information a manipulative man needs to run game on you. Again, I'm not assigning blame; I'm attempting to provide you with enough truth that you can take responsibility for the way you are treated.

I'm not Like Most Guys

I'm literally laughing out loud at the thought of a man having the audacity to make this claim. If a man is not like most guys, then you will see it well before he has to say it. When I was in the military, periodically a leader would proclaim his rank in an attempt to remind his subordinates that he is in charge. Effective leaders never did this. They never had to tell you they were in charge; it was a well known fact by the way they carried themselves.

But why would a man say this? Probably because you told him about your frustration from dealing with whom you've identified as "most guys". Now, you've made him aware that you've been hurt and that you're a little skeptical about his intentions. The reality is that anyone who has dated as an adult has experienced rejection, pain, and disappointment. So why are you laying all this information at his feet. By informing him of all the bad things that most guys have done, you are providing him a blueprint for what not to do to win your affection. Although it may seem like a productive way of getting treated the way you want, it isn't coming from an organic place. He's not being the opposite of most guys because he is; he's being the opposite of most guys because you told him what most guys did. Again, this is your date not your therapist. Allow him to present his true self without your assistance. Tell him what you like. Tell him what you enjoy doing. Tell him all the places you enjoy going. Keep your past relationships to yourself. His behavior should be genuine and not just a fabrication created by your horror stories of past relationships or dates.

Timeo Danaos et dona ferentes

This Latin phrase loosely translates to, "Beware of the Greeks bearing gifts." For non-history buffs, in the battle of Troy, the Trojans mighty wall was breached by the Greeks with what would eventually be known as the Trojan horse. The Greeks built a huge wooden horse and presented it to the Trojan army as a token of surrender. The Greeks sailed their ships away from Troy and the Trojans, believing they had defeated the Greeks accepted the gift and brought in into their impenetrable walls. The same night, an elite group of Greek warriors spilled out of the wooden horse and defeated the Trojans who thought the battle was over. The subterfuge served as a valuable lesson; not everyone bearing gifts is your friend.

A very big part of the game is gifts, overt acts of kindness, and a hastiness to use pet names. You have to ask yourself why a man you barely know would go out of his way and go above and beyond for you. Be careful of the so-called "nice guy" usually these aren't nice guys at all. These men are often times very insecure and they try to buy your affection by being overly accommodating. In the end, if your affection isn't returned the way they see fit, these guys will turn on you quickly. I mean seriously, how can you be someone's "baby" or "angel" and he doesn't even know your middle name? A man should do nice things for you or refer to you with terms of endearment because of your unique qualities. You should insist on earning his affection and be very leery about receiving this type attention too soon.

Compliments are one thing but be careful with men who seem to overdo it. The world is a big place, are you really comfortable with being considered the most beautiful woman in it, especially before the first date? A man who shows restraint in this area should be a welcomed suitor. The reality is that you probably are the most beautiful woman he has ever seen; however social maturity will temper his desire to proclaim this notion to anyone within shouting distance. Besides, is your beauty the only thing you want a man to covet? Shouldn't he be equally enamored with your intellect, personality, and other non-visible qualities?

I know a woman who was showered with compliments and gifts by a man she met on a dating website before they even had their first date. She admitted that she enjoyed the attention immensely. He texted her throughout the day and never missed an opportunity to tell her how beautiful she was and how lucky he felt to get the opportunity to get to know her. On their first date he took her to an expensive restaurant and insisted she ordered the most expensive thing on the menu. He picked her up in a limousine. He showed up at her door with a dozen long stem roses and the next day, he had another dozen delivered to her home. She thought that she had found a gem and couldn't wait to share her excitement with me. Her excitement was short-lived when I insisted she be a bit more pragmatic. I simply asked what she had done or said to earn this level of adornment. She dismissed me as a hater and informed that she was happy that she had finally met a man who knew how to treat a woman.

I received a call a few weeks later from my friend letting me know that my skepticism was well founded. First, he tried to move their dating relationship into something more physical before she was ready. When she declined, he got angry. He reminded her of all the gifts he had given her and all the money he had spent on her. He insisted that she owed him a physical encounter that was equal to his financial investment. When she made it clear that she owed him nothing, he warned her that she would never find a man like him and that she was about to lose the best thing that ever happened to her. She cut communication with the man but was still a little shaken up by the encounter.

I took no pleasure about being right about my assessment of the guy, but I did insist that she learn from the ordeal. No one will pour resources into anything without expectation. Having expectations without taking the time to get to know someone is silly. She allowed herself to be charmed by his adoration and didn't take time to learn his true intentions.

There is absolutely nothing wrong with receiving gifts or acts of kindness from a man. As a matter of fact, if you enjoy that type of thing, I think you should seek out men who enjoy giving gifts and being kind. However, everything should be commensurate with the time you've spent together. You see, the goal is to be the reason he does special things, not just the target. His compliments should be believable and his gifts should illicit feelings of gratitude, not shock and awe. Don't misread this as advice to settle for a cheap man. Instead, a suggestion to date a man who places value on a woman he has taken the time to learn is valuable. I can almost bet my paycheck that right now some other woman is being courted in the same aggressive and manipulative way my friend was.

The Slick Talker

Ah, the slick talker. This, I have to admit, is my favorite tool of the game. I'm surprised how many women fall prey to a man who is able to talk in circles. In my youth, I employed these tactics and I was quite successful. The slick talker displays a certain level of confidence that is admired by women and men alike and it is not without merit. He exudes a self confidence that appears to be an excellent quality. Here's the rub. Most slick talkers are not confident at all. They are just master manipulators. The slick talker will say things a woman wants to hear whether he believes it or not. Often it sounds a bit rehearsed because it is. His conversation is almost poetic in its delivery. He knows just what to say because he's said all it before to other women who fell for his lines.

I know... I know... you are way too smart to fall for that. I'm sure you are. The slick talker knows this and will adjust accordingly. He's a natural high-pressure salesman employing the same tactics any salesman uses to close the deal. You're not a deal and the goal shouldn't be to "close you" but to get to know you.

So how do you know you're dealing with a slick talker? Simple, slick talkers don't ask a lot of questions because questions don't allow them to control the conversation. Slick talkers make statements. They tell you what you're thinking so that you align your thinking with their words. Slick talkers know how to make you get comfortable with saying "yes". The few questions they do ask are usually going to be answered in the affirmative. As yes continues to flow from your mouth, soon you are being manipulated into affirming things you are not really comfortable with. It's an art really. The slick talker rarely reveals anything meaningful about himself but he will tell you stories of how he's been hurt. He will put you in the position to save him. He knows that it is in a woman's nature to nurture so he will make you comfortable with building him up. He's self deprecating but only for the purpose of making you his cheerleader. He wants you to save him because then he can make you feel as if he is in your debt. Once you're convinced he needs you, he knows you'll do anything for him. He loves to speak of "we" and "us" as if the two of you are a team and of course, you're the captain. The slick talker uses your past as a means to separate you from anyone or anything that may reveal his true intentions. The slick talker will attempt to monopolize your time so that his voice reigns supreme. By the time you realized you've been manipulated, it's too late. He's got you!

Avoiding the slick talker is simple. Stay true to what you want. Make yourself a priority and *the* priority. It is not your job to save anyone. If you meet a man with issues, allow him the time to deal with those issues and insist he deals with them without you.

Ask questions! Force a man to speak on the fly and not from a rehearsed playbook. The easiest way to throw a slick talker off his game is to share control of the conversation. The only way to uncover or counteract game is with truth. You don't have to be skeptical of every man you meet, but certainly be cautious. Take your time to get to know him and abandon any urge you may have to save him. You can't and you shouldn't. Sincere men are cognizant of their flaws and they only reveal the mistakes that they have corrected or are attempting to correct. Unless you are dating a psychic who has proven his abilities, no man should know what you are thinking – even if he's spot on.

The game is best suited for women who display levels of desperation. It doesn't work on confident women who know what they want and refuse to settle. As a matter of fact, the more you know about yourself and your desires, the sillier the game will appear when it is presented to you.

If you are a poor communicator that is often misunderstood, take the time to improve your communication skills by talking to trusted advisors. Family and friends that you've developed relationships with can help you speak your mind freely because they have a vested interested in what you are feeling and what you have to say. Ultimately, your intuition is the strongest communication tool you have in your possession. Learn to pay attention to yourself by investing in yourself, just as you are. You know exactly what you want so don't be manipulated into taking anything less!

END OF CHAPTER HOMEWORK

Honestly assess your communication skills. Do you routinely feel misunderstood or feel that you have a difficult time getting your thoughts out? Is it easier for you to say what you're thinking or do you prefer writing down your thoughts?

Take an assessment of your preferred method of communication. Do you like to text or do you prefer phone calls?

Do you value a man's ability to speak in complete sentences are you okay with "text speech?"

If you do participate in online dating, when are you comfortable taking your communication from the computer to a more personal tool like the telephone?

How often do you expect to communicate with a suitor? Do you want a text every morning or are you okay with days going by without hearing from a man you're dating?

Make the decision to carve out time to communicate with someone you are dating. Even if you are busy, mentally set aside appropriate or ideal times that you can communicate with a man with minimal interruptions and distractions.

What is it that you want to know? The worst question is the one you don't ask. Although every conversation shouldn't feel like a job interview, there's nothing wrong with having prepared questions that you think will help you determine whether or not a man is suitable for you.

Be conscious of what you intend to share and at what pace you intend to share personal information about yourself. Remember, don't treat the dating process like a therapy session. Your past hurts should be reserved for someone who has earned your trust.

Take a mental note of instances in your past that a man has or has tried to run game on you. What made you susceptible? At what point did you realize you were being manipulated? What is your plan of action if it happens again? Remember the sooner you recognize a master manipulator; the less damage he can do with his manipulation.

Finally, be relentless in your desire to be approached the way you feel is the "right way" and don't settle for anything less! People will either rise to the standard you set or they will avoid you if they cannot. Make sure a man knows who is dealing with from the introduction.

THE INCREDIBLY FRAGILE MALE EGO

If a man thinks he's not conceited, he is very conceited indeed. –
C. S. Lewis

I find it interesting that in the thousands of pages of biblical text, in both the old and new testaments, not one of those pages instructs a woman to *love* her husband. Men are told to love their wives, but women are not given that charge. It's strange because the nature of a woman is to love...hard! There is nothing more powerful in this or any universe than the deep, passionate, and consistent love of a woman for a man. So why did the bible leave those words out when it comes to how a woman should feel about her man?

In all actuality, the bible didn't overlook telling a woman to love her husband; it just says it in a different way. Women are commanded to *respect* their husbands.

R-E-S-P-E-C-T

As a man I can tell you a few truisms about men that could apply to a solid majority of us. The most consistent attribute amongst a wide variety of men is the desire for respect. Respect, not sex, is how we receive and recognize love. Let that sink in for a second. It isn't your body we crave but your respect, your adoration, and your admiration. I should feel like *the* man because I am *your* man.

Does that mean a man expects you to fall to his feet and shower him with praise? No… not exactly. Respect comes in many forms and often times disrespect is displayed in the most benign and unknowing ways. Women I know have complained that they were accused of being disrespectful to a man, and they are honestly clueless about when or how she did it.

I have a buddy named Craig who has been dating a young lady named Denise for about a year. All Craig talks about is Denise and how much he truly loves her. About nine months into their relationship, Denise received a promotion at her job and began reporting to a new boss. Within two weeks of her promotion, Denise began speaking about her new boss more frequently and with growing admiration. Craig started confiding in me that he was getting sick of hearing about her new boss. Almost every day, Denise would tell Craig about some smart thing her boss had said or some brilliant thing he had done. Her excitement for working with someone she truly respected was rubbing Craig the wrong way.

Now Craig didn't believe that Denise was sexually attracted to her boss but he did feel uneasy about her constantly lauding him with praise. He asked me what he should do and quite honestly, I was stumped. You see, I didn't think Denise was attracted to her boss either but I understood where Craig was coming from. We both agreed that confronting Denise the wrong way would give Craig the appearance of being jealous and irrational. He wasn't jealous of Denise's boss, just jealous that he wasn't the subject of her excitement.

We consulted a mutual female friend, Lacy who knew Denise well. We hoped she could provide us some insight before Craig confronted Denise. To our surprise, Lacy found our insecurities extremely humorous. She informed us that she and some of Denise's other friends had the same complaint about the way Denise went on and on about Craig! She told us that when Craig wasn't around all Denise could talk about was; "Craig said this and Craig said that." As recent as a day before our conversation with Lacy, Denise even mentioned to her female friends how much she wanted for Craig to meet her new boss because she thought they would have so much in common.

What bothered Craig about Denise's admiration for her boss was his belief that she *only* admired her boss. Just as she probably never told her boss how great she thought he was to his face, Denise failed to affirm Craig face to face. I encouraged Craig to have a conversation with Denise with this newfound information in the back of his mind. Eventually, he informed me that she received his concerns well and promised to do better at making sure that he could hear her praise.

I want to be very clear; a man should deserve your veneration because he has worked to earn it. The fruits of his labor in his professional development, personal endeavors, and his treatment of you should be plain to see. Not just any man deserves your reverence. Once you've decide to make him your man, then he certainly should hear or at the very least, feel your adoration. You see, it's all about titles. If you happen to be a believer, then you know that your Lord and Savior sits high in your life above all others. Those titles and the unwavering proof that He has earned those titles make it easy for you to worship Him in spirit and truth. Do not underestimate the title, *my man*. Those words denote ownership and choice. You chose to be in a relationship with this man and if has earned that position then show him the respect the position deserves.

You are a prize for a deserving man. You should feel like a prize and in return, so should he. Imagine a relationship where he showers you with love and in turn, you shower him with respect! Sounds great huh?

Well what if he doesn't deserve my praise?

Then you need to ask yourself why you are with him. I take you back to the dating process and its extreme importance. The dating season is when he vies for your respect and his consistency throughout this process is the reason he should eventually earn it. If you can't respect him, then you shouldn't be with him and you certainly shouldn't commit yourself to him for life. I am shocked at how many women have honestly told me that they knew after the first or second date that the man they are still with was not the man for them. There are a host of reasons why each woman continued to stay, but the reality is that she is unhappy and so is the man in her life. She doesn't feel loved and he doesn't feel respected; and so they continue in this merry-go-round with no end in sight.

Fragile; Handle with Care

The male ego is fragile. Even the most confident and self-assured man has insecurities. I can safely make the generalization that most if not all men judge their worth by the visual manifestation of their efforts. The job he has, the shape of his body, the car he drives, and even the woman he chooses are ways that men define themselves. I'm sure you've even heard a man say that he wants to "get his stuff together" before he gets serious about a woman. You see, we have a desire to bring something to the table that will garner your respect. We want you to look upon us with a sense of security that shows us that you feel safe with us. A man who does not see himself as complete will never be able to show love because he can't justify earning the respect of a woman.

I know gentle reader; I know exactly what you're thinking, "I don't care about material things; I just want to be with him." I get it. Logically, it makes sense that you would think or say that. You are a nurturer. Even more so, I've already illustrated how your presence in his life could be the key to the success he craves! So how do you overcome the male ego and earn a man's trust? Respect.

If you can find a reason to admire him in his building phase, he will welcome you in as a partner as he builds. This isn't just about words of affirmation; this is about you having the ability to look upon this man and see the same potential for greatness he sees and the greatness that he currently possesses that escapes his sight.

I'll let you in on a little secret: A man who won't commit isn't always scared of losing his single status. Often times, these men are not ready because they don't feel complete. These men have a tendency to focus on how much further they have to go than reveling in how much they've accomplished thus far. In your valiant effort, you attempt to *love* him ferociously, hoping he'll see his worth. Hasn't worked yet has it? As a matter of fact, I'm willing to bet that the more you love, the more he pushes you away! He doesn't understand your love because he doesn't feel he deserves it. However, if you were to pull back on the love a bit and increase the respect… prepare your mind to be blown!

So what do I mean by respect?

Seek his council on personal decisions. You don't have to take his suggestions, but soliciting them communicates that you respect his mind and his ideas.

I know *submit* is a dirty word in our feminist culture, but submission has power if you are submitting to the right man. Pick and choose what you are willing to submit to and then do so without hesitation.

While you are picking and choosing, do the same with your battles. Being *right* doesn't mean you've necessarily won. It just means you're right. What's the value of being right all the time? Be selective in your arguments and reserve your will to fight for those topics or subjects that you feel passionately about. Let go of all the trivial, inconsequential stuff.

Be mindful of your praise towards other men. When a man's name is constantly coming from your lips, your man will quickly feel intimidated regardless of how innocent the relationship is. We tend to go towards our focus and the things we say are a good indication of that focus.

Let him pay. I know a couple that does this whenever I join them for dinner at a restaurant. They are in a long term relationship and have maintained separate bank accounts. When they go out on the town, they take turns paying to keep things even. However, before the bill comes, she will take her credit card out of her purse and slide it to him. When the waiter arrives with the bill, he gives the waiter the card. It seems trivial but she respects his desire to remain in the traditional role, even though they have a very progressive relationship. Let him pay.

Be mindful of his abilities and allow him to ask for help, even if you suggest it. Hey, don't laugh… I told you the male ego was fragile. I have a family member that violated this concept with horrible results. Her boyfriend, a man she had been dating for almost a year, needed tools to work on his motorcycle. She has a neighbor that converted his garage into a mechanic shop. With good intentions, she informed her neighbor that her boyfriend would need help with his motorcycle and asked if the neighbor would come by and give her boyfriend a hand. When the neighbor showed up at her door to help out, her boyfriend reacted in a very predictable way. He needed the help; she had access to the means to provide the help he needed; however she didn't consider his ego. A better way to handle that situation was for her to make introductions and allow her boyfriend to seek the help he needed.

I AM NOT ABOUT TO SIT HERE AND STROKE SOME MAN'S EGO

...and that's your choice. Maybe you will get lucky and find a man who is so sure of himself that his ego is in check. Good luck with that.

I am not suggesting that you engage in any behavior or take any actions that contradict your values or beliefs. If you think the above suggestions are too regressive then by all means, don't do them! You shouldn't feel a need to do anything that makes you uncomfortable. That doesn't change the fact that most men have very fragile egos, me included. I don't require all of the above suggestions, but a few might make me feel a little more secure in my relationship and increase my desire to show love to the woman who made these small sacrifices.

Ego vs. Self Esteem

Now I've spent a lot of time talking about ego, but let me make sure I explain the difference between ego and self esteem. It is not your job to build anyone up. Self reliance, self assurance, and self esteem are based on self. You cannot create worth in a man that doesn't see his worth. You cannot create value in a man that doesn't see his value.

If you find that the man you are dating needs constant affirmation, this isn't ego; this man has deeper issues and I caution you strongly to steer clear of him. Self deprecation can be exhausting to witness and detrimental to be a part of. Your man should need reassurance that his self image is authentic. He should be reaffirmed that he is as good as he thinks he is. Even if you are a counselor or therapist by trade, your date is NOT your patient.

END OF CHAPTER HOMEWORK

Take a moment to honestly consider your ability to be mindful of a man's ego. How far are you willing to go to affirm a man so that he feels respected?

Does this notion of respect violate any of your personal beliefs or values?

Has it backfired in the past? If so, can you honestly say the man actually deserved your respect?

What are ways you are willing to show respect and admiration? What are ways you are unwilling to?

CONCLUSION

You didn't ask and I'm not qualified, but I hope my words resonated with you on some level at some point throughout this book. I hope you have a man's perspective on dating and a tool of self reflection that has allowed you to empower yourself and re-enter or continue in the dating world with confidence, boldness, and the unwavering belief that you deserve uncontrollable happiness!

If you've been completing the homework after each chapter, you should have a pretty extensive list of your needs, desires, and limitations. Review this list before you go out in social settings and before you agree to the first date after meeting a new guy. I firmly believe the merit of Habukkuk 2:2:

And the LORD answered me, and said, Write the vision, and make it plain upon tables, that he may run that readeth it (KJV). Run, dear reader, run boldly in the direction of your heart's desire and be uncompromising and unyielding to what you truly want out of life and love.

My deepest and most sincere desire is that one day there comes a point where you truly see your worth and the worth that men see in you. I wish that you could feel the butterflies that are in our stomachs when we finally convince ourselves to approach you with sincerity for the purpose of finding out if your immense beauty is deeper than your pretty face. Even if you don't struggle with feelings of doubt or struggles with self worth, I hope you understand that you still don't give yourself enough credit –

and you should. You are truly God's greatest gift to the universe.

I'd like to share with you, with her permission of course, a friend's text message to me when she finally decided that she was worth more than what the man she was dating was willing to give. Without apology, she let him know in very plain language, that she could no longer sacrifice her value for the possibility of his love.

Please enjoy her unedited proclamation:

Doing some self inventory. Trying to be a better person and parent. About to make some changes so I can reach goals I've set for my kids and me. As far as us, I don't think the arrangements are healthy for me. I'm not that person. I like labels. I like to know where I stand. I like to be romanced and sent flowers for no reason. I like to know I'm missed or loved or appreciated. I'm not all about sex. I've compromised myself because I was so happy to get some attention and to have sex on a regular basis. But I want more. I want to be trusted. I want to be relaxed and feel like I can bare my complete self with someone. I want to be vulnerable and protected. This past 13 months has been a rush and quick fix to a long term problem. I miss being married. My husband was my best friend. He didn't judge or criticize. He loved me unconditionally. I could be my whole self with him. I'd rather go without sex for another five years if it means I'll

find someone to make me feel whole again. I want someone

to help me raise my girls and engage with them and give them a sense of security and love.

You're a smart and admirable man. You're a wonderful father. Your dedication to your daughters reminds me of my dad. I want that for all of my girls someday. But I can't keep acting like I'm the person who is fine with this, whatever kind of "ship" we have. I'm not a "just friends" person who has casual sex. I'm a "monogamous relationship, working towards something long term, wants someone who loves God, me and my children like his own", person. You've made it clear that you're not that person so I feel it's time to end things. I have not been with anyone but you since May 2010. I'm not with anyone now. I'm not looking for anyone now. I'm trying to get my kids settled, get my finances under control, finish school and hopefully find a job that allows me to work from home. We can be platonic friends if you want. It's all up to you.

Made in the USA
Coppell, TX
07 December 2019

12562699R00085